B.S.

BOWEL STIRRING THINGS

A Natural History of Mental Laxatives
& the Bowel as Predator Detector

Russell Kightley

Paperback edition, 2026
ISBN 978-0-6451595-8-5

With thanks to family and friends
for their suggestions and support.

Canberra, 2026

Contents

1996–2026

THIRTY YEARS AGO, in 1996, I finished a book about things that stir the bowels. It took over two years to write and was the culmination of a quarter century of thought and discussion. The bound manuscript lay unread and unloved for thirty years, yet its insights quietly informed many aspects of my life—and the lives of some around me. It is time to reopen *Bowel Stirring Things*.

Let us return to 1996:

Introduction

THIS BOOK is about bowel stirring things, those thoughts and situations that agitate the guts and bring on an urge to run to the toilet. It is a voyage into a strange world of mental laxatives, where ordinary things shimmer with hidden monsters.

It is well known that extreme fear can loosen the bowels, but the topics covered here seem much less threatening. Some have traces of fear or insecurity, like the common urge to visit the toilet before a journey, but most seem safe enough. For example, some people find that browsing through a second-hand bookshop, making a telephone call, or viewing old farm machinery stirs them into action. The *Fantasies* section contains a wide variety of bowel stirring (or B.S.) imagery that proves this point.

An extraordinary variety of objects, places, arrangements, and thoughts can trigger the B.S. Some contain elements of comfort juxtaposed with elements of discomfort, such as an armchair in a street. In others, there is an unexpected or surreal combination of objects, as in some modern art. If you are stirred by such things, you might dismiss the effect as a quirk—something deeply personal that is best ignored. However, having considered the subject for many years, I am convinced that the effect is not idiosyncratic but general. Moreover, I believe it is an inborn and ancient response, a view explored in the *Origin* chapter.

Whatever its genesis, the B.S. is a strange and exotic thing with great utility. It can be an amusing and devastating instrument to analyse architecture, industrial design, telecommunications, art, and works of fiction in all media. Conversely, it can spur creativity and generate ideas. Indeed, it sometimes seems to me that B.S. techniques are widely used in the creation of certain objects, books, films, and television programs, simply to make them more compelling.

The B.S. can also spice up conversations, giving them a delicious air of conspiracy and making them seem quite profound. Most basically, though, the B.S. gives you power over your bowels. Using the B.S., you can trigger the urge to defaecate almost at will and thereby relieve constipation or save time in the toilet. You can timetable your motions around trips or work schedules and so avoid potentially embarrassing situations. You can evacuate yourself before venturing into a world of dubious public toilets.

The B.S. can be highly amusing, but it takes a certain kind of courage to introduce the subject to others. You need a sense of diplomacy and timing. It helps if you are a good judge of character too. Don't try it on a first date.

Unhappily, not everything about the B.S. is positive. It is important to understand that this bizarre urge to open the bowels can be overwhelming, especially in someone who has only recently been introduced to the technique. While the urgency can be easily handled at home, it can be appalling if it occurs somewhere else. Unfortunately, the B.S. can be triggered virtually anywhere by a stray thought or a funny circumstance. If this happens, you can find yourself fighting to stay continent in the street, park, opera, or marketplace. You might be with your boss, a customer, or (perish the thought) the object of your desire, and few things could wreck a career or douse the fires of passion more effectively than an explosive bowel motion in company.

Knowing that the B.S. can operate on a hair trigger could tempt you to provoke the feeling in somebody else. This is a very wicked thing to do and great mischief can be done, especially if the victim is miles away from a toilet. Self-interest alone points against using the B.S. as a weapon, for it can backfire horrifically. You might stir your own bowels into violent ferment and leave your victim quite unmoved. Alternatively, the person chosen as the butt of this joke might be more skilled at the techniques than you, and so deliver a swift and fluid retribution. If this happens, you might find yourself locked in a B.S. arms race, with increasingly outrageous descriptions being exchanged. Such competitions can end very badly if there is only one toilet available. Two people who are exploring the B.S. together should come to an agreement to avoid using the techniques maliciously on one another, tempting though it might be. Fellow travellers will need to develop an etiquette that preserves dignity. Once the ground rules have been set, though, it can be a great journey to undertake in company.

Fantasies

B.S. FANTASIES are musings that bring on the urge to evacuate the bowels. They can have elaborate plots or be little more than mental tableaux. These small daydreams help you relax and have an easy bowel motion. They might work instantly, but it is more likely that you will need to persevere for several weeks before any result. To make them more effective, try replacing the times and places that I have chosen with details that have personal significance for you. Use these fantasies as a starting point to create a private gallery of bowel stirring images that you can browse whenever you feel the need (but not the urge).

The Spaceship

Whilst locked in the toilet, you can construct (in your mind) a perfect spaceship. This craft is a safe and completely self-contained world, perhaps based on your own home or an idealised version of it. The whole point is to house everything that is comfortable and important to you in a vessel that is impenetrable to your foes and never wears out. You can build and decorate the most wonderful rooms in this ship—a great wood-panelled study heavy with books, charts, and various devices, or a workshop with all of your favourite tools and equipment. Imagine orbiting the Earth, sitting in your favourite armchair, surrounded by your library, and gazing out at the hard emptiness of space through a simulated sash window. Skim the surface of Loch Ness, or hover above the trees of the Amazon rainforest. Imagine such a vessel parked in your back garden, just waiting for you to finish loading it with your favourite pieces of furniture, ornaments, and records.

The Partially Built Lorry in the City

Imagine that you have a lorry that consists only of the drivetrain and chassis, with the driver's chair perched at the front, totally exposed. Dressed in a heavy coat, you must drive this open-work vehicle down the back streets of the industrial area of Birmingham. You pause to pick up some friends who must cling to the chassis, since there are no seats...

Tending the Distant Garden

Imagine that you own a small front garden attached to someone else's house. The house, like the others in the terrace, stands close to the pavement and has a bay window. All day people walk past the garden, giving it little thought, except, perhaps, as a convenient rubbish dump. An old honeysuckle, surely placed there years before, sprays up the wall and drapes across the brickwork. It is 3 o'clock in the afternoon of a spring day, and you have just arrived on your old bicycle with your gardening tools in the saddlebag…

Touring a Deserted Hospital on a Monorail

Imagine an abandoned hospital that sits on a peninsula that juts into a lake. The car park is empty except for a couple of old cars. A few people are still working in scattered offices around the campus. You enter by the old emergency exit. Turn left and walk down a wide and long corridor. Take the lift to the third floor. When you step out you notice that a monorail has been laid along the centre of the corridor. A small steel chair is perched on top, like an inverted ski lift. Climb onto the chair and pull the start handle to your left. The chair surges forward, powered by a small electric motor strapped to its underside. You pass trolleys and drip stands, open doors leading onto deserted wards, and noticeboards with tattered papers pinned to them. So far, the monorail has been bolted firmly to the floor, but now it turns a corner and the supports are attached to the wall, leaving you completely clear of the ground.

Nearly Meeting In a Hotel

Imagine arranging a peculiar rendezvous in a hotel. You organise things so that you and a friend stay at the hotel at the same time but never meet. You could arrange not to meet for dinner by booking the same table at different times or distant tables at the same time. The whole enterprise is more bowel stirring if the hotel is far from home. Perhaps two Englishmen could arrange not to meet in a hotel in Tasmania.

The Toilet that Straddles an External Wall

Imagine a toilet that stands in a hole that has been knocked through an external wall. When sitting on this toilet, you will have one foot in the garden and the other in the utility room. Looking straight ahead, you see the cavity between the inner and outer skins of the brick wall. One side of your body is warmed by the air coming in from the nearby kitchen, whereas the other side—projecting into the garden—is lashed by a cold wind. The cistern is bolted to the outside of the house and the chain swings in the wind. The toilet paper is dispensed from a free-standing holder, positioned in the middle of the garden path.

A Personal Computer in a Public Space

Imagine keeping your computer—with all your letters and confidential files—in the foyer of a large hotel or museum. Visitors could browse through your private material and might even add items of their own. You have work to do on the machine, so you pull up a chair and type away with your back to the crowd.

The Bus Shelter Connected to the House

Imagine a bus shelter directly in front of your house. A small-gauge railway line starts in the middle of your sitting room, runs through an archway set in the bay window, across the front garden, over the footpath and into the bus shelter. A wooden chair with wheels, powered by a small electric motor, allows you to chug back and forth between your comfortable living room and the bus stop in the street.

It is 8.30 at night. You are sitting on the motorised wooden chair in the bus shelter, out in the street, reading a book. A car squeals around a corner several blocks away. Someone approaches along the path. It is time to slip the little lever into reverse and quietly retreat back into your living room. The last thing you want is a nosy passenger asking awkward questions about the small-gauge railway connecting your house to the bus shelter.

A Private House in the Middle of a Campus

Imagine owning a house that stands in the middle of the quad. It is a conventional two-storey home surrounded by a low picket fence. During the day, students walk all around it and lean against the fence. At night, the campus is very quiet and your house is far from any other dwellings. You feel the urge to scan the campus with night vision equipment.

The Model Aeroplane

Imagine that you have a remotely controlled model of a WW2 bomber. The plane is about 3 metres long and its bomb bays can be used to transport various objects. Video cameras are located fore and aft, where the gunners would have sat. Pictures from these cameras are transmitted to your remote control console to help you fly the plane. The plane has an incredible range. Refuelling depots exist at strategic points around the world, giving the plane unlimited reach. These are also controlled from your console. Now imagine a series of tasks that the plane must do. You could, for example, carry a book to a relative who lives on the other side of the world. You load the book in through the bomb doors, where it is clasped by mechanical arms. You plot a rough course for the plane. You could fly by electronic navigation, or simply use the video cameras to fly by visual cues alone. Take the plane to a local place that can act as a runway. Perhaps a nearby park or a quiet stretch of road. A night take off along the high street would be ideal.

The Old Radio

Imagine trying to hunt for stations on an old valve radio. It is 10 o'clock on a Friday night in November. You are in a back bedroom of a terraced house in Northampton. The radio stands on a table next to the window. An Anglepoise lamp illuminates the work surface. Above the table are shelves weighed down with books and old copies of *Wireless World*. Jammed between the books are several electronic meters and an oscilloscope. Wires spill down from them. The room is strewn with dismembered television sets and other electronics.

Through the dusty window, you can see across several walled gardens and the roofs of the houses and garages. The night is cold and overcast, although the odd star is visible. Look at the radio. The valves glow faintly. You turn the dial. Static. Then comes a snatch of music from a distant orchestra, some singing, and finally a cultured voice reading foreign news. The reception is poor, as if the messages are actual sounds trying to reach across huge distances in the night.

The Railway Carriage in The Museum

Imagine owning a railway carriage that sits in the foyer of a transport museum. It contains all the comforts of home such as a settee, a bookcase and a standard lamp. From the outside, it's just another exhibit. You retreat there after the day's visitors have left. As the museum lights go out, the other exhibits loom menacingly. The only light is from street lamps. Draw the curtains across the carriage windows. Try to forget the ghostly dark of your immediate surroundings. Remember, your telephone (an old Bakelite one) connects to a socket outside your carriage. Anyone prowling around the museum could unplug the cord...

The Train

Imagine owning a railway carriage whose interior is furnished like your living room. From the outside it looks dirty and unprepossessing, and no one suspects it's your refuge. You can park it anywhere on the rail network. It is highly secure, so you can safely leave it in the sidings while you explore beyond the station.

Imagine a series of carriages containing various rooms of your house. One is your lounge, left in a siding in Northampton. Another houses your library, and is parked at New Street Station in Birmingham. Your bathroom and toilet are concealed in the guard's van kept at St Pancras Station in London. All of these carriages are connected by telephones whose cords plug into sockets just beneath the lip of the platform.

The Fireplace in the Street

It is a dank and drizzly night in the village of Medbourne. You are sitting in an armchair in the street, facing an old brick garden wall. Your chair is perched on the grassy verge and tips back slightly. Three feet in front of you is an arched fireplace built into the wall. It has been disused for decades and water pours through the grate, making it impossible to light a fire. You have to make do with a small paraffin heater. The arrangement is made more homely by a row of ducks hung above the mantelpiece. Gilt-framed pictures of farming scenes, interspersed with the odd portrait, hang on the wall. Some are only a few inches above the grass, while others are well above head height. They are dotted along the whole length of the wall, some thirty yards on either side of the fireplace, and even continue around the corner. It gives the impression of a huge living room unfolded and erected in the street, the roof having collapsed into a line of coping stones. A nest of occasional tables completes the effect and keeps your cup of coffee clear of the water running along the gutter.

The Tower Block with a Crane

Imagine a tower with a crane fixed to the top. The crane stretches from the roof towards the ground. At the end is a metal chair. Controls on the chair can manoeuvre it anywhere in the sphere reachable by the jointed arm of the crane.

The chair is suspended two feet above the lawns that surround the tower. Climb in and steer the chair so that it skims over the grass.

Teleportation

Imagine being able to teleport anywhere. This is very B.S. You can playfully exit the safety of your bathroom and visit all sorts of hostile places. The B.S. is stronger if teleportation depends on a machine because you might lose the device, have it stolen, or be denied access. For example, you might use a torch-like device to teleport. When you arrive at your destination, you have to wait ten minutes for the power supply to recharge. Put the torch down while you go exploring, knowing that some-one might steal it in the meantime. Even if it's still there when you return, its batteries might fail to recharge, leaving you stranded.

Visiting the Office Whilst Invisible

Imagine visiting your workplace at a quarter to five on a Thursday afternoon. You are completely invisible. The secretary continues typing as you walk past. You creep over to the boss's office to check that it is clear. You can hear the other workers leave, one by one. The secretary sighs, shuffles her papers and puts on some lipstick. Tip-toe back, making as little noise as possible. Lean over her shoulder and stare into the make-up mirror. She shuts the mirror, pops it back in her handbag and looks up at the clock. Exactly five. She scans the room to make sure that everything is in place. For a moment she looks right through you. Then leaves, locking the door behind her.

Go to her desk drawer to find the key to the locked red filing cabinet. Back in the boss's office you pull your personal file. Take it into the corridor and squat on the floor. Read it carefully in the middle of the carpet. Anyone watching would see a file whose pages slowly turn by themselves. Check the reference you were given for the last job that you applied for. Return to the main office to copy it. Switch on the photocopier by the door. It makes a huge noise, like an aircraft taking off.

The Decrepit Entrance

Imagine a rotting wooden door set into an ivy-covered brick wall. The bricks are ancient with warm red hues. Open the door and look into the garden beyond. It is large and quite formal. Flower beds are arranged in a radial pattern, with pathways converging on a central fountain. You enter and carefully close the door behind you. The air is very still, trapped by the brick wall that surrounds the whole garden. The sun beats down and the air is heavy with the perfume of flowers. The drone of bees makes the place seem even more peaceful.

The far wall has a greenhouse built into it, the roof nearly reaching the coping stones at the top. Inside, vines hang down, heavy with grapes. Another door is set into the wall on your right. Go through the door. This section of the garden, once formal, is now overgrown. This region feels alien but familiar. Peculiar things blossom, and deep, impenetrable undergrowth covers the ground.

Strange items of garden furniture are dotted about. Statues, fountains, ponds, and brick walls crop up here and there. There are arches to walk under and ruins to explore. It seems deserted but it resonates with a magical force. The remains of a series of fish ponds, fountains, and waterfalls lie half concealed in the undergrowth. The lawn is more like a meadow, and there are wild flowers everywhere. In the distance, seventeen old trees, placed in an oval, shade a small horse that nibbles the grass.

Owning Bookshelves in the Local Library

Imagine owning three lengths of shelving in your local public library, where you store some of your favourite books: a metre-long section near the entrance where people look for new releases, an entire top shelf in the mysteries section, and a bottom shelf in the far corner of the reference library upstairs.

You could enjoy your books at any time, perhaps sitting in one of the comfortable reading chairs that are scattered about. The other users would never suspect that you were consulting a private library embedded in a public one.

Library books can be transferred to your own shelves, where they can stay for a couple of weeks. You can take books belonging to you, or the library, home. However, they must be checked out at reception.

Imagine borrowing a novel at half-past ten in the morning and stashing it in your shelf in the reference section. You return at half-past nine that night. It is drizzling and miserable outside. You open the main doors using your private key and quickly reach round for the light switch. As the doors slam shut, dozens of fluorescent lights flicker on revealing the vast deserted foyer. The eye-pummelling strobe effect soon settles down and a cool thin light fills the cavernous library.

During the day, light would filter in through the tall windows. The foyer would have figures hunched over newspapers and a small but steady stream of borrowers taking out their reading matter. But now the daylight and the people have gone.

Take off your damp coat and hang it on a coat hook. Lean your umbrella against a table. Directly in front are the dark stacks of the lending section. To the left, a grand marble staircase sweeps up to the reference section. Climb the stairs. Pause half way up. Lean on the cool balustrade, wide enough to sit on and smooth enough to slide down. Look down across the darkened mass of books on the ground floor. Listen carefully for any sounds. Nothing but a distant motorbike droning along the High Street.

Continue climbing until you reach the wide landing. Switch on the lights for the rest of the staircase. Prints of the old town and its surrounding countryside are lit up. Continue up the stairs, pausing to look at the old tinted pictures. The reference section is behind a partition of wooden panels and windows, through which the collection of reference works is just visible. Unlock the door and enter the reference section. Switch on the lights. Choose a large wooden table near the entrance and put your notepad and pencil on it, then go over to your private shelf in the corner. The surrounding shelves hold ancient multi-volume encyclopaedias and old editions of guides, directories and almanacs. Stoop down and retrieve the novel that you secreted there earlier in the day. Go back to the desk near the door and start to read. Every hour, break off and consult the old encyclopaedias for the project you are working on.

The Double-Decker Bus & The Canal

It is 11 o'clock on a Wednesday evening in early December. You are standing on a quiet road by a canal. On the other side of the canal is a factory, dank and deserted, whose walls rise straight from the water. The bricks at the bottom are filthy, covered in slime and crumbling. On the other side of the road is a scrap yard. A gantry straddles a mountain of cars like a slowly feasting dinosaur. Street lamps march past the scrap yard, one of them picking out a mindless scrawl of graffiti on the corrugated iron wall. A distant car accelerates away, its gear changes sounding like intakes of breath.

An ancient double-decker bus is parked by the canal path. This bus has been heavily modified. All of its controls are remote, for the driver's seat is projected from the driver's cubicle on the end of a crane, like a mutant eye on a stalk. The seat hangs above the canal, clear of the oily water by only a few inches. A joystick on the seat controls its height above the water as well as its distance from the bus. The driver's foot controls have been replaced by knobs, like those on an old radio. The steering wheel is still there, though. It has a handle projecting up, so that it can be turned with one hand. Cables, rods and chains connect the chair to a machine bolted to the upper deck, where the front seats would normally be. The machine is housed in a grey painted metal box with rounded edges. Dials and switches of unknown utility face backwards down the deserted aisle. From the right of the machine, armatures project and attach to a series of rods that pass through a hole in the upper deck. They enter the driver's compartment and work the foot pedals, brake and steering column.

It is extremely B.S. to control this bus from the external driver's seat. The air is cool and damp and clings around you. A small electric fan heater bolted near to your feet tries hard to warm you up, but most of the hot air is just lost into the night. By careful manipulation of the joystick you can position the chair several yards from the canal bank and a few inches above the water. Using the knob controls, you cause the bus to creep along the road at slightly less than walking pace. No one else is around. Even the bus is empty.

The Flying Armchair

Imagine that you own a magic armchair that can hover around or fly great distances. Overstuffed and covered in one of those prints that look like heavy ferns uncoiling. A comfortable but unlikely flying machine. It is surrounded by an invisible barrier, like the glass bubble of a small helicopter, that stops freezing winds and rain.

One cold November night, you decide to take it for a flight. Carefully steer it out of the lounge and into the hallway. You have to get up to open the front door. Park the chair in the front garden for a moment while you lock the front door and gather your thoughts. Then it is time for lift off. A slight tinkle as the castors, like unre-tractable undercarriage, drop a fraction of an inch. Ascend in a tight arc. Bank sharp left and get a glimpse of your porch and then your roof and then your desolate back garden. Settle three feet above the top of your house.

Look back down the line of roofs with their damp slates glistening in the moonlight. Imagine that you can see through the slates, felt, rafters, joists and ceilings and into all the little rooms. See all the lives lived out there, partitioned from one another forever.

Straight ahead, along the line of chimney stacks, lies a church steeple, like the final sight on a long gun. It stands on the corner by the traffic lights. The only car out tonight is sitting patiently behind the red light. They turn to green and the car drones off towards the park. To your right is another church, its squat tower back over your right shoulder. The church rooms, currently being renovated and extended, are to your immediate right. Evidence of building work lies strewn about; a small cement mixer, several heavy duty planks and assorted tins. Scaffolding clings to the brickwork.

Track along the rooftop of your neighbour's house, which is the last one in the terrace. At the end of the roof, pause and look down the sheer wall of bricks. The corner of the block is occupied by an all night service station. Hover out across the forecourt. The garish signs light up the corner and it is rather like cruising over a factory or industrial complex that has been lit up for security reasons. Pass under the canopy as if you were about to fill up with petrol. The petrol pumps stand impassively like metal guards. Swoop out and over to the roofs of the houses in the next block.

At the junction of each house with its neighbour, you have to divert around a chimney stack. After doing this four or five times, peel off left and fly above the back gardens, every now and then going right down until you are hovering only inches above someone's lawn.

Now fly north, across the back gardens opposite, over those houses, several more blocks, round a steeple of yet another church and then hang twenty feet over the main road. Look down at the closed shops. There is a chemist on the corner, a little supermarket further, a television shop and an off-licence. Turn left, and hover about thirty feet above the road. Follow the white line in the middle of the road until you come to a set of traffic lights. To your right is a corner pub, shut for several hours now. Go up and have a look at the sign, which is in the shape of a circus elephant on its hind legs. Spend several minutes inspecting the sign, paying particular attention to the fluorescent tube that follows its outline and the tiny cracks and marks in the paintwork. Look over the bricks to the slates on the roof.

Now rotate the chair so that you face a park opposite. It is a deep velvety black. Swoop down to the lawns and pause a couple of feet above the damp grass. Climb out of the chair and wander about. You are standing in the middle of a huge expanse of grass. It is skirted by roads and looks like a dark lake with houses around the shore. The chair bobs about behind you, like a rowing boat. A line of street lamps marches across the middle of the park, their weak lights tracing a footpath like a slim bridge across the expanse of blackness. It is a path that no one in their right mind would walk down at this time of night.

Return to the chair and head for the path. Now hover along it at walking speed, two or three feet in the air. Finally, you reach the edge of the park. Land the chair and cross the road on castors. This is slow and quite noisy.

Elevate to six feet and continue along the road opposite. To your left is a grammar school and behind that a technical college. Playing fields behind railings. Next comes a high school. A modern looking place with a tower of classrooms. Go over the railings, over the bike sheds and up to the main entrance. Now simply rise slowly, pausing at each floor to look into the deserted classrooms. When you reach the last floor but one you remember that you have left your front door open…

The Flying Mechanical Chair

This is a high-tech version of the flying armchair—a pilot's seat without an aircraft. On each arm are joystick controls that guide the chair. Various mechanical devices replace the "magic" of the armchair. Smaller than the flying armchair and highly manoeuvrable, it can easily navigate through the interiors of buildings. Unlike the magic armchair, which can never go wrong, the mechanical chair can break down, run out of fuel, or get lost.

Imagine keeping the chair in your garage on a purpose-built metal frame. All the tools to maintain it are hung up neatly. There is a workbench with a jointed lamp. And for when you have done all the work, a small armchair to rest in, and a radio on a shelf to listen to.

Tonight, everything is quiet. The chair is in perfect working order, and full of fuel and oil. It's the ideal night for a flight. Open the garage doors and climb into the seat. Make a final check of all the instruments. There are clusters of small round dials, like watches. And imposing meters. And counters. And funny little tubes with purple liquid, like swollen thermometers. All the readings are normal. Press the small green button on the left arm. The chair starts to vibrate softly, rises with a whoosh, then settles six inches above its stand.

Take hold of the joysticks and guide it carefully through the garage doors and out into the cobbled alleyway.

A street of motley garages stretches in both directions. Most of the sheds are poor old things, sagging and leaning on each other for support. The one next door is new and brash, like a teenager. The moon is three-quarters full, lighting the clouds like ribbed sand on a beach. It's a cool night, threatening rain once more. A good night to visit the museum in the park…

You sweep down the alleyway, the chair pitched slightly forward so that you can watch the cobblestones rush by. Across the road and into the next alley. This one is wider and less familiar. Slow down, angling the machine to the right but keeping on straight ahead. Inspect each garage door in turn. Most are rickety wooden things, but there is the occasional metal up-and-over model. It's difficult to tell what colour they are in this light, though.

One more alley to go and then you emerge into the sodium-lit main street. Bear right, then skim above the complex of traffic lights and roundabouts at the edge of the park. Fly over the bus-shelter-cum-police-station just inside the park and head for the lakes. No one is feeding the ducks at this time of night. Just as well really, since you plan to hover out across the water and have a look at the island.

Go once round the island, then back across the park, over the road lined with trees that separates the two halves of the park, and up to the museum that stands next to the church. Dead, blank stone, dank and forbidding. All the windows are dark, giving no hint of the exhibits inside.

Climb to the second storey and glide along until you reach the window whose catch you unlocked earlier in the afternoon. A mechanical arm from the side of the chair prises the window up and you fly inside. It is very dark and you can only just see the outlines of large display cases. Switch on the small lights on each arm of the chair. The beams sweep the room revealing the stuffed owls, swans, and pheasants all in frozen imitations of life.

The chair rumbles slightly. Swing it round and steer it through the door. In the corridor looms another huge case full of stuffed birds—faded and ghostly. An ornate wooden chair stands near the doorway. Climb off the flying chair and sit on the museum chair for a moment. Your chair rocks slightly, its lights picking out the massive oil portraits that hang on the wood-panelled wall. Glass eyes and oily eyes watch you as you sit down in the dingy passage.

Walk into the next room. Headless mannequins wear old-fashioned costumes. Uncomfortable looking underwear, hats, and gloves lie in glass cases. Peer into the corridor.

The flying chair is still hovering a foot above the floor-boards, like an eerie museum exhibit gone walkabout.

You think you hear movement in the costume room. Rush back and jump in. Grab the two joysticks and gun the chair to the wide stairs. Suits of armour standing in unconscious guard flash in the chair's lights. Swoop down the staircase. Pull around to face the stairs. A huge portrait glowers at you from the landing. Everything seems very still.

Tiptoe out of the chair and pull the huge bolts on the front doors. Swing them wide open. There is definitely some movement from upstairs. Run back and grab one of the arms. No time to clamber in. Drag it into the court-yard and lever yourself in. The chair wobbles gently, just clear of the gravel. You sit there panting for a few seconds.

Pull the controls fully back, so that the chair rises verti-cally. Once you are level with the museum roof, look down at the entrance. One door slams shut. It's time to go.

The Desk in the Street

Imagine standing on a street in Northampton, a town in the English Midlands, at 9 o'clock on a Tuesday evening in early October. The air is damp and clingy. Terrace houses with bay windows run all along your side of the street. Across the road, the terrace is broken by a garden wall with a workshop built into it. Sodium street lamps march off in both directions casting an alien yellow tint. The tarmac is damp and dimly reflects the street lights.

A large office desk straddles the kerb in front of you. One set of drawers stands over the pavement and the other above the road. The work surface is scarred and polished, with heat rings from long-dead coffee cups. Behind the desk is an adjustable metal swivel chair. The leather upholstery is torn and the stuffing is getting damp. The backrest is broken and lies at a strange angle, like a fractured limb.

An umbrella is bolted to the desk in a futile attempt at shelter. An office lamp emits just enough light to read by. A single bar electric fire glows under the desk. The wires from the lamp and heater pass through a crack in the front door of the adjacent house.

Your task is to sit at the desk and write a letter, but first you must retrieve a pen from the house.

Open the door and follow the wires from the fire and lamp. Walk along the hallway. The first door on your right opens into the sitting room. Step inside and you will see an overstuffed settee and two matching armchairs. They face a cold fireplace. Little figurines cavort on the mantelpiece. On the back wall is a huge oil painting in a gilt frame. It shows a Highland scene with cattle. Chains suspend it from the picture rail. The painting makes the room seem heavy and still, like a museum reconstruction of a family room.

Return to the passage. Directly ahead you will see the staircase rising to a gloomy landing. Continue along. Another door opens on your right. You glimpse the side of a piano. A glass-fronted bookcase fills one corner. Walk down the passage. On your left is the wood panelling of the staircase and the balustrade.

The end of the passage opens into the breakfast room. Step inside. There is an armchair in the far corner, with a library book lying face down on the cushion. A gate-leg table stands under the window. It is set for supper with cheese and biscuits and a jar of pickle. A teapot, covered in a knitted tea cosy, releases a thin coil of steam into the still air. There is nobody around. A clock ticks on the dresser. The kitchen beyond looks dark and deserted.

Return to the hall. The cellar door is now on your right. Open it and turn on the light, so that you can follow the wires down the steps. The air smells damp and dusty. The cellar is dimly lit by a naked bulb. A wooden chair stands in the far corner. The window at the far side is at street level and admits a faint yellow light.

To your left is a partition with a sash window set into it. The panes of glass are grimy with coal dust. This window has had a poor outlook for eighty years. Shelves with tins and bottles are just visible through the window. The wires snake across the cellar floor and into the little room. Follow them. They plug into a socket near the entrance.

There is a fountain pen and a bottle of ink on the middle shelf. Grab them and run up the cellar steps, down the passage, and out into the night. Sit on the broken office chair. Reach into the right hand drawer for some paper. Now write a letter to a friend or relative who lives abroad. A van grinds along the road, but the occupants ignore you.

When you have finished your letter, bend down to the drawer at bottom left (8 inches above the tarmac) and pull out an envelope. There are some stamps in the top left drawer. When you have sealed and stamped the letter, all that remains is to post it in the pillar box at the end of the street. Having done that you can go back into the house to see if the tea is still warm…

Origin

IT IS WELL KNOWN that fear agitates the bowels and some B.S. things, such as a haunted house or an alien spaceship, are scary in an obvious way. However, most bowel stirring things seem quite innocent: an armchair in the street, a rotting car on a pole, the start of a journey, or an open-plan office. The B.S. is full of everyday objects that look familiar and should feel safe. They may be arranged oddly, or be in unexpected places, but they lack any obvious malice. Even the imaginary machines that crop up in B.S. fantasies seem harmless enough.

But bowel stirring things contain a buried germ of horror. Comfortable B.S. situations echo a primal threat. It is simply a matter of decoding the scenes and recognising the objects and arrangements as symbols of something fundamental and sinister. The B.S. disturbs us with deep-seated fears, not obvious ones.

The B.S. allows fear and relaxation to coexist and reinforce each other. These two feelings would be expected to cancel each other out, but in the B.S. they operate symbolically. Consequently, the paradox of being scared and relaxed remains hidden. The two bowel stirring emotions work on the guts together, and their action is spiced up by a dim recognition of their contradiction.

Many aspects of the B.S. seem to be rooted in childhood fears and experiences. This topic is dealt with in *Childhood & The B.S.*, but it is important to emphasise the point now in order to make sense of the reasoning behind *Predators & The B.S.*, which depends on the B.S. response being inherited.

Predators & The B.S.
The B.S. is linked to fear and feels deep-rooted. To make sense of it, I had to find an ancient and serious threat. Predators were a good place to start, since they are nearly as old as life itself. As soon as I looked at the B.S. in terms of attacks from other creatures, everything fell into place.

The techniques that animals use to avoid predation have amazingly close parallels in the B.S. They include avoiding infested territory, detecting predators, avoiding exposed territory, running away, and finding a safe haven. Apparatus might also be used, including armour, weapons, camouflage and mimicry.

Avoiding terrain that might harbour enemies means knowing what constitutes potentially infested territory and recognising places where predators might lurk. This really means looking for characteristics of a territory that make it attractive to a predator. One obvious feature that would appeal to a predator is an abundance of hiding places. Consequently, a measure of the number of potential hiding places could indicate how dangerous a place might be. This would help to explain why a deserted city feels so threatening (see *Empty City B.S.*). Boxes, chests, wardrobes and other containers large enough to conceal a predator might be B.S. for the same reason.

Detecting predators is more complicated than just recognising the hallmarks of predator country, for predators might venture into what is normally safe territory. It is crucial to recognise the traces they might leave—to see when a potential enemy has modified the environment. This means noticing strange juxtapositions, things that are not there by chance, unexpected arrangements that suggest that an intelligence has been at work in the vicinity. These signs are likely to be very subtle because predators rarely want to advertise themselves (unless intimidation is used as a strategy). Consequently, the most minor shifts in an otherwise normal landscape are enough to set off our built-in anti-predator alarms. This could explain why outdoor sculptures or ancient ruins can be unsettling. Crop circles too might agitate us because they are like giant footprints. Some predators hunt in packs and this might explain why certain groupings of objects stir the bowels. Several objects of the same kind that stand in a regular formation might suggest a pack in disguise. Perhaps some sculptural layouts are effective for this reason. Likewise, groups of similar machines can be very B.S.

Running away involves identifying escape routes and maintaining mobility. If the B.S. is an ancient survival mechanism, it must continuously scan the environment for escape routes. It must avoid leading us into dead ends (literally in this case). Things that might impede escape, or exert a pull towards the predator, create a deep agitation in the bowel and help us evade them before they threaten our safety.

Finding a safe haven is crucial. Having run, one must hide. Many things seem to trigger the B.S. because they imply refuge. The mind is continually trying to identify bolt-holes, secure places that will allow us to relax. Bowel stirring things almost invariably contain a refuge of some kind. The B.S. impels us towards these safe havens and dissuades us from leaving them.

These behaviours alone are persuasive evidence of a predatory genesis, but the B.S. also seems to contain correlates of predator-prey apparatus. That is to say, those parts of animal bodies that are designed to attack, or to help ward off attack, seem to have been transformed into symbols that are important to the workings of the B.S.

Armour can render a structure more B.S. by making it safer from attack. Roofs of houses can be B.S. for this reason and slates might be reminiscent of scales or scutes. A building that looks like a tortoise hunched against the elements can be inviting in a B.S. sort of way. Equally, armour might suggest a fighting creature that we should be wary of.

Certain weapons might induce a tingle in the bowel. This chiefly occurs in weapons that look like they might fail. The B.S. seems to be warning us not to rely on such devices for protection. The B.S. seems to recognise that the sense of security that these weapons offer is false (see *Unreliable Machine B.S.*).

Camouflage can make a person or refuge less obvious and therefore safer from attack. Disguising powerful abilities, potent machines, or secure buildings beneath unimpressive exteriors creates a B.S. tension (see *Hidden Power B.S.*). The extreme version of camouflage is invisibility. Fantasies of trespassing while invisible are highly bowel wrenching. As well as being a mechanism to evade predators, camouflage is also used by predators to avoid detection. Consequently, when we see something that has been disguised, we might suspect that it is a predator attempting to sneak up on us. Like so many things in the B.S., camouflage seems to have a dual role.

Mimicry is allied to camouflage, but rather than just disappearing or hiding, it involves passing off as something else. A machine that looks like one thing but is, in fact, another. An example would be a telephone handset that looked like an iron. Predators use mimicry as well. See *Wolf in Sheep's Clothing B.S.*

It is reasonable to suppose that many symbols in the B.S. relate to both predators and prey. After all, the hunter and the hunted are locked into a competition in which similar techniques will be used by both sides. It is this recognition that things can be used for defence, as well as attack, that gives so much ambivalence to B.S. symbols. It might partly explain the coexistence of relaxation (when the item is defensive) with agitation (when it is used by the enemy) that is one of the hallmarks of the B.S.

It is important to emphasise that the B.S. operates at a barely conscious level and that the threats are now largely symbolic. They might once have given timely warning of a predator, but now they have been transfigured into archetypes. By recognising these deeply embedded symbols, we can explain why displaced pieces of furniture, telephone boxes, empty offices undergoing renovation, rusty tractors, and dusty attics all distress our bowels. There are no obvious references to enemies or predators, only oblique hints. There are no guerrillas, lions or sharks hidden away, but something subtle in the environment has caused us to react as our forebears might have reacted to the predators (now long since disposed of) that stalked them. It seems that when we have a bowel stirring reaction, we are triggering an ancient anti-predator device into activity.

A person in the grip of the B.S. suffers from a paradoxical mix of agitation, fear and relaxation combined with a heightening of the senses. This turbulent amalgam suddenly makes sense when we remember that someone who suspects that a predator is nearby will feel distressed but, in order to survive, must remain sufficiently relaxed and receptive to pinpoint the source of danger and navigate a safe exodus.

Natural Disasters & The B.S.

Non-living threats also occur in the B.S. These include darkness, storms, floods, fires, earthquakes, collapsing ground, and collapsing structures. Such inanimate threats cannot be pacified or outwitted (see *Lightning Conductor B.S.*). In this respect, they are reminiscent of hostile and implacable machines: they cannot be reasoned with, and so escape or shelter are the only options. However, unlike predators, they do not evolve to catch up with our improving escape methods. Forest fires and earthquakes are terrifying in their scale of destruction, but they do not become more dangerous.

Inanimate threats may be detected by subtle environmental clues: a slight change in the weather might suggest a flood, a crackle of wood might suggest a fire, or minor structural deformations might suggest an imminent collapse.

A feeling that something is wrong with the landscape could prevent us from being caught up in a landslide or rockfall. A creaking noise could frighten us from a tree that is about to collapse or lose a bough. Perhaps creaking floorboards in an old house elicit the B.S. because their sound is reminiscent of such a tree. Derelict buildings can be full of structural danger signs that tug on the colon (see *Unsound Structure B.S.*).

An ancient fear of thin ice might explain the modern bowel stirring response to open-work floors such as metal mesh walkways and piers with gaps between the planks (see *Skeletal B.S.*). The ultimate B.S. floor would be made of glass.

Many of these elements, such as electrical storms, tumbledown castles, and darkness, appear in Gothic fiction. Haunted houses are usually rather decrepit, and in these situations *Unsound Structure B.S.* compounds the fear of supernatural beings (see *Gothic B.S.* and *Supernatural B.S.*).

Many B.S. fantasies use mild versions of natural disasters. Rain and fog, for example, are sufficient to spice up a scene, but they are too mild for us to recognise as being related to natural disasters. Like the attenuated trace of a predator, they cause a response, but they are too weak or altered to be recognised consciously.

Childhood & The B.S.

Many features of the B.S. seem childlike, and it is surprising how many childhood experiences have counterparts in adult B.S. These include crawling around and inspecting things, visiting strange and frightening places, getting lost in large public buildings, hiding behind furniture, hiding in boxes, being pushed around in a stroller, and building small shelters or playhouses. So potent are childhood things for inducing the B.S. that, as adults, we might use an imaginary time machine to regress. Under stress, we yearn for simpler things and may inspect details in an attempt to recover a childlike perspective.

The attributes of childhood may be linked to the B.S. for several reasons. Children may experience the B.S. more easily because they do not analyse things as much as adults do. As we grow up, the B.S. reflex fades and the old survival mechanisms become buried beneath the weight of education and training. By remembering childhood, we can recapture a more imaginative and sensitive state and so reactivate the old anti-predator device.

Memories of early incontinence and toilet training might cause adults to associate bowel motions with childhood. As we practise the B.S. as an adult, we might recall the context in which we first learned bowel control. Children may be pressurised to evacuate their bowels before leaving the house and such messages could lodge at a very deep level, generating *The Travelling B.S.* later in life.

A major characteristic of childhood is security because a child has parents to ward off danger. Childhood is perceived as a refuge, and that causes the viscera to tingle. However, the important thing to remember about children is that they are vulnerable. Young animals are often preferred by predators, who try to separate them from the herd. Consequently, things that make us feel small and vulnerable can trigger the B.S. This is another example of how apparently opposite things work together in the B.S. Childhood is a potent mixture of refuge and vulnerability.

Some of the activities are listed below:

An Interest in Details.

One obvious characteristic of the B.S. is an interest in fine detail—a concern with the physical reality of objects rather than their perceived value. To a child, the most commonplace object is a source of fascination. Children prod and poke and inspect things from all angles. To them, everything is full of magic and worth a good look.

This interest in the detailed structure and surface appearance of everyday objects fades with age. By adulthood, most people verge on a state of sensory deprivation. They are aware of the utility, financial value, and prestige of objects, but tend to miss their physical appearance. This is one reason why many adults are incapable of drawing. Training in draughtsmanship can help restore the ability to see things more directly and appreciate the objects themselves, not just their associated values. The ability of artists to observe the world in this innocent way partly explains why so many works of art are B.S.

An Interest in Things at Ground Level.

B.S. activity frequently includes inspecting things at ground level. There is an interest in floorboards, skirting boards, carpets, and the small detritus found there. Children notice things at ground level far more than adults do. Their whole world is several feet below ours. They are quite happy to scrabble around on the floor and they spend a good deal of time playing on the carpet. This fascinating realm is normally overlooked by adults. Most would never consider crawling around on the floor to look at things. Even if the thought crossed their minds, they would probably be too embarrassed to act on it. Unfortunately, an adult operating at ground level looks cumbersome and undignified and can become a figure of fun.

Activity at ground level is B.S. because it recalls childhood, but there are other explanations as well. The sense of scale is different at ground level, and distances seem greater due to the shift in perspective. For humans—who presumably evolved from arboreal stocks—being at ground level means greater exposure.

Building Little Houses.

The B.S. often features small shelters, and children are forever building little places to hide in.

Children enjoy playing in small shelters, whether fully fashioned toy houses or simply a few cushions and chairs piled together. These places, which are too small for adults to enter, act as refuges inside the parents' house (see *Embedded Building B.S.*).

Getting Lost.

Feeling lost is very bowel stirring and a constant fear. It can reactivate memories of being separated from parents during visits to shops or zoos (see *Separation from the Herd B.S.*). For a juvenile in the wild, separation from its parents can spell disaster.

Moving Chairs.

Memories of being pushed around in a stroller or pushchair may resurface as thoughts of flying or mechanical chairs. Carrying shopping home in a pushchair may echo in later life as an urge to carry objects around in imaginary vehicles. Rocking horses and swings may lay the seeds for impeded mobile chairs.

High Chairs.

For a child, being perched conspicuously in a high chair can be unsettling. Being strapped in intensifies *Sitting B.S.* These feelings may persist, generating a bowel-tumbling response to elevated seats later in life.

Skeletal Containers.

Memories of being in a playpen or cot may cause open-work structures to be B.S. in later life (see *Skeletal B.S.*). Looking through the bars of the playpen at the lounge room, the child may feel restricted and exposed, like being in a cage.

The B.S. power of a playpen can be illustrated by imagining a flying playpen in a deserted shopping mall. You take various items with you—a couple of your favourite books, a flask of coffee, and a camera—and guide the device around a department store, occasionally stepping outside the playpen to collect items from the shelves.

Collecting Things in Childhood.

Children often enjoy collecting and arranging objects. Collecting and cataloguing occur in the B.S. (see *The B.S. & Collecting*).

The B.S. has certain obsessional qualities. Collecting objects from a wide range of sources, cataloguing information, and framing and displaying the results are very popular in childhood, but less so later in life (see *Art B.S.* and *Framing B.S.*). In children, such activity helps make sense of the world and classify its contents. However, collecting things also echoes stocking up before a siege or journey (see *Ark B.S.*).

Childhood as Refuge.

Childhood is seen as a time of security. When we recall our early past, we enter a mental sanctuary that gives welcome relief from the stresses and uncertainties of adulthood (see *Time B.S.* for a discussion of the contrast between the certainties of the past and the uncertainties of the present). A nostalgic yearning for the parental home and all its comforts can tingle the belly. Like so many attributes of the B.S., childhood refuge is juxtaposed with its opposite: childhood vulnerability.

Childhood Vulnerability & The B.S.

Baby animals are more vulnerable to predators than juveniles or adults. Consequently, situations that make us feel childlike can be bowel stirring. Unusual proportions, perspectives, or atmospheres give us the impression that we are looking at things through the eyes of a child, which is disconcerting. However, like almost everything else in the B.S., it is too subtle to be recognised consciously.

Things of an unusually large scale make us feel small. This is particularly true of interiors. High windows, high ceilings, and large pieces of furniture give us the perspective of a child. Rooms remembered from childhood seem monumental and cavernous, rather like the inside of a church. In large public buildings, we may be stirred because the rooms resemble greatly expanded domestic spaces. This is especially true when they are dotted with furniture from the home: a three-piece suite lost in the huge atrium of a hotel, a cooker in the corner of a warehouse, or a bookcase in an aircraft hangar.

A still atmosphere and a sense of mystery can make us feel childlike. Stillness reminds us how slowly time passed when we were young, and the sense of mystery recaptures our childish confusion at an incomprehensible world.

To a child, things that adults take for granted can look alien. Revisiting childhood is unusual and unsettling; its bowel stirring response is a fearsome nostalgia for a magical period mixed with a terror of being small and vulnerable.

Predators, Natural Disasters & Childhood

The B.S. might originally have formed part of a survival mechanism that helped to protect our ancestors from attack—a device tuned to detect dangerous creatures and identify escape routes, like a mental radar continuously probing the environment. When something untoward was detected, it triggered discomfort in the bowels. The B.S. was a background activity—a constant scanning for telltale patterns. Huge amounts of information had to be processed and decisions made quickly and accurately—an instinctual response to danger signals. We could get on with our lives while the system kept guard.

A bowel stirring response that was developed against predators would take inanimate threats in its stride. Non-living hazards are simpler and cannot evolve, whereas predators are likely to become more sophisticated. Avoiding both animate and inanimate dangers involves detecting subtle environmental clues, planning escape, and recognising and assessing refuges. The refuges against both types of threat are similar: a cave to escape a storm, an island in a lake to avoid a forest fire, a tree or a piece of high ground to escape a flood.

Non-living threats also increase exposure to hostile animals. For example, darkness conceals nocturnal predators, while structural instability—the potential loss of support—can threaten sudden exposure. This can happen when a branch gives way and drops us on the ground. As well as exposing us, the sound of the crashing branch can alert predators. Earthquakes, fires, and collapsing ground might also force us into the open, where we are easy prey (think how fire drives game out of the forest).

Childhood experiences fit neatly into this scheme, for play may rehearse and strengthen innate B.S. abilities. Hide-and-seek, building little houses, and even diving onto the floor, may hone our B.S. sensitivities. These games might have had great survival value in the past. Now they provoke a strange tingling in the bowels and, because of this thrill, are repeated.

In summary, the B.S. seems to be the remnant of an extremely fast and sophisticated pattern-recognition system that evolved as a defence against predators and then expanded to warn of inanimate threats. It is an inherited device that continues to be reinforced by childhood play. It detects and attempts to solve problems that are not obvious to the conscious or rational mind. It continually monitors the environment for subliminal threats, plans escape routes, and notes the location of refuges.

The bowel stirring sensation is essentially a warning signal that something is wrong. The tumbling of the guts alerts us to danger and to some extent points the way to safety. If something looks hostile, ineffective, liable to collapse, or if a threat is suspected, or a prospective escape route is blocked, or a potential refuge is dubious, then we get an urge to defaecate, and in our discomfiture we turn away. The twinge in the bowel can be strong enough to stop us in our tracks and force us to seek refuge. If we are already safe, but the B.S. has detected an external threat, then it immobilises us while we assess the risks. At the same time, it helps us empty our bowels in preparation for the difficult time ahead, when we have quit the refuge and would be hindered by a bowel motion.

The B.S. echoes the "gut feeling" that people describe when they are uncomfortable but cannot pinpoint why. Interestingly, when we operate at an almost intuitive level to quickly navigate through hazards, we call it "flying by the seat of our pants".

The B.S. Today

The B.S. seems more suited to life in the wild than to modern society and, being anachronistic, it sometimes fires unexpectedly. Modern situations—which have no direct counterpart in prehistory when the mechanism evolved—can trigger feelings that vary from a mild tingle in the guts to an overwhelming and irresistible urgency.

Long after its immediate survival value has diminished, the B.S. continues to make its presence felt. Before leaving home, many people still experience an overwhelming urge to visit the toilet. Nowadays, with so many safe toilets around, this *Travelling B.S.* is more of a hindrance than a help, but we cannot shake off our past. As we contemplate going to work in the hostile city, we might imagine the little toilet that awaits us at our office: the modern equivalent of the clump of trees near the horizon.

It is possible to consciously control the B.S. and convert it into something quite novel. Someone well-versed in B.S. techniques can trigger the sensations at will and develop a unique set of bowel stirring ideas. New and sophisticated types of B.S. can be formulated that are far removed from the survival forces that shaped the original device. In these modern varieties, the urge to defaecate becomes weaker. There may be a residual twinge in the guts, but the whole enterprise becomes more cerebral. This pure and sublime form of the B.S. becomes a visceral appreciation of the world. The bowels act like an internal sense organ, responding to special contrasts that lie hidden from normal view.

When we understand this aspect of the B.S., we can create artworks that stimulate our bowels in a pleasurable way. There is nothing outrageous in conceiving such an art movement because all art is appreciated via the senses, and the senses evolved as survival devices. The fact that our eyes were not produced to gaze at great paintings, nor our ears to listen to symphonies, is not an argument against producing such works. The B.S. is like a new sense and so it can spawn a new art.

Although the B.S. can be customised and vary from person to person, there will always be a shared core. These common aspects of the B.S. could be exploited by the media, for they may be as compelling as sex and violence, but they can be used covertly (see *The B.S. & Subliminal Persuasion*). If this is happening, then *B.S. Art* is already well developed.

The next section is a tongue-in-cheek illustration of how an early human may have first noticed the B.S. It will crystallise some ideas about the origin of the B.S.

The Landscape of Potential Toilets

Imagine an ancestral human gazing across the open ground from a safe place behind an old tree. A shoreline or savannah stretches in front of him. He is cautious before venturing out from the forest in case he is caught short far from cover. He knows that defaecation leaves him vulnerable to attack. Smells and sounds might alert predators or enemies, and his mobility is reduced, making him an easy target. He could be spotted by a lion or a rival when attending to himself.

So he scans the land for potential toilets, little islands of security that he can run to if he is caught short away from the safety of the forest. These refuges might be caves, clumps of trees, or piles of rocks.

Identifying these safe locations is useful, but it would be far better if he could relieve himself in the forest. Unfortunately, the urge isn't there. His heavy brow furrows as he considers the problem. If only he could be the master of his bowels and void them in safety before venturing into the exposed territory. He stands paralysed by indecision. He must cross the open ground but is fearful of leaving the protection of the trees.

As he contemplates the contrast between the safety of the forest and the exposure of the plain, and visualises the quickest routes between the potential toilets that he has identified, something stirs deep in his belly. A connection is made. Recognising the link, he tries again. Concentrating hard, he fills his mind with a complex model of the landscape, criss-crossed with escape routes, dotted with potential toilets, and colour-coded according to degree of exposure. The slight stirring becomes an overwhelming urge to empty his bowels. His brow relaxes and a childlike smile spreads across his face. It is the glorious dawn of the B.S. for this happy man.

He now becomes an opportunistic defaecator, able to take advantage of safe places as he finds them rather than be hostage to a capricious bowel—for his bowel might know when it is full, but only he knows when it is safe to evacuate. He is also better equipped for hunting. Not wishing to be distracted by a full bowel during the chase, he can now void himself before leaving home.

However, the B.S. provides more than a simple easing of his motions. Since he has to repeatedly visualise connections and patterns in his environment to trigger the feeling, his powers of imagination and analysis improve. He wants to tell everyone about his magical new ability and insight, but he lacks the skills to do so. His friends look on, mystified and aggravated by his frequent bowel motions and smug expression. His new-found interest in small details and peculiar natural formations is incomprehensible to them, for they are not privy to his thoughts.

Elders surely place his behaviour down to youthful enthusiasm, for even if it were explained to them, there would be no guarantee that they would understand. (Indeed, it seems that sensitivity to the B.S. may be lost with increasing age and that older people find the whole idea extraordinary.) Future generations may discover the technique for themselves, but since it is not discussed, there will be no formal recognition of the phenomenon, nor any cultural transmission of it.

Some Advantages of The B.S.

The first and most basic advantage of the B.S. is that you can improve your ability to induce a bowel motion. This is convenient if you need to go before a journey or before guests are expected to arrive.

The imagination can be exercised by creating *B.S. Fantasies*. Directing these mini-dream sequences will help stimulate creativity.

The B.S. gives critical insight into art. Analysing the Art World in terms of *B.S. Theory* is amusing and iconoclastic. You will be surprised at how the most arcane pieces can be categorised and explained. Whether the artwork is an assemblage in a museum, an outdoor sculpture, or an odd conceptual piece in a corridor, the B.S. can explain them.

The B.S. could add interest and appeal to designs. Architects might incorporate B.S. features into new buildings or oversee restorations that generate *B.S. Tensions* between the old and new. Interior designers might create bathrooms whose features ease the motions of those who visit them. Landscape architects might lay out gardens that are impossible to wander round. Advertisers might use B.S. images to intrigue and captivate potential customers. Industrial designers might dream up household appliances that bestir the gut, such as vacuum cleaners with overtones of industrial machines, or washing machines that tumble the guts. Furniture designers might create bowel-achingly B.S. chairs and bureaus.

Artists might use B.S. techniques to dream up compelling new works.

The senses can be heightened almost at will. This alertness, originally for danger, makes the world seem more intense. This is thrilling and part of the intoxicating pleasure of the B.S. As your guts make the most mundane scenes jump out in high relief and new relationships reveal themselves, you will wonder at how flat the world must seem to those unschooled in the B.S. It gives you the chance to see through a child's eyes again.

Things and Categories

THIS SECTION covers major categories, including buildings and machines. It begins with *The Travelling B.S.*, as many people experience a tumbling of their bowels before a journey.

The Travelling B.S.

This is the familiar and intense urge to visit the lavatory before a journey. The longer the trip, or the more hostile the route or destination, the more powerful the feeling. It may originate from the urge to pre-emptively void the bowels before venturing into hazardous terrain. Or perhaps the B.S. warns you against leaving because the journey is too risky. *The Travelling B.S.* may be combined with constipation when away. Some people suffer from both effects and can timetable their motions to occur at home.

The effect can be heightened by pottering around the house beforehand. This re-acquaints you with your rooms, and so makes the leaving more of a wrench. It is a good idea to include places like the cellar, attic, and garden shed in the tour. People generally wander around in an upright posture to scan the house before leaving, but a much better idea is to get down on your knees and elbows and shuffle around in the *B.S. Posture*. This tumbles the bowels and allows you to view things at ground level. Try looking at the wallpaper near the skirting board, where a small crevice is often visible and older layers of paper fan out like the pages of a book. Wallpaper can be very B.S. because, try as you might, you cannot take it with you. When deeper and older layers are visible the strain is greater. Look for scuffs and scratches on the skirting and floorboards and inspect the frayed edge of the carpet. All sorts of tiny objects might be visible, such as scraps of paper, bundles of dust, hairs, grit, and pieces of grass. Proceed around the room in this fashion, comparing the sensations that different regions of the skirting board provoke. Have a good look under the sideboard, at the back of the television, and behind the settee. If you are brave enough, carry on out into the hallway and have a good look around the foot of the stairs. Occasionally, you can look up to view the door furniture, coat-hooks, light switches, and ceiling lights (which can repay a good look from such an unusual angle). Do not forget to inspect the electrical sockets, door stops, and telephone wires. Spending a few minutes down the cellar with your bottom in the air should finish things off nicely.

By crawling around the floor in the *B.S. Posture*, things can be appreciated at a scale of inches or even fractions of an inch. This contrasts sharply with the scale of things on the journey, which are viewed more in terms of yards or miles. Quietly contemplating items on the floor might also bring to mind childhood memories of playing unconcernedly amid the bustle of adults organising a trip. If constipated, you might relieve the situation by pretending that you are about to go on a journey. So, if all else fails, adopt the *B.S. Posture* and imagine that your international flight leaves in a couple of hours.

Architectural B.S.

Buildings are steeped in the B.S. Much of childhood is spent indoors and so early B.S. experiences often involve buildings. Trips into the outside world, with all its hazards, normally start by leaving a building. Buildings are full of details (see *Detail B.S.*) and may have many memories associated with them. Above all, they are refuges. Unfortunately, any refuge can also conceal an enemy, which creates uncertainty (see *Refuge-Trap B.S.*).

People live and work in buildings, and an occupied building is normal and comfortable. Consequently, when part or all of a building becomes vacant, all sorts of strange impressions may arise.

Empty Room B.S.

An empty room in an otherwise occupied and furnished house can be very B.S. Such a room can feel like a part of the outdoors that has been incorporated into the house. This is most likely to occur when a room is being decorated. If the windows are left open to help the paint dry, the room gets colder and more disturbing. The acoustics and appearance become harsher when the wallpaper, curtains, and carpet are removed. This scraping back of layers can trigger *Dissection B.S.* If the curtains are missing, then the room seems naked and exposed. An occupant will be visible through the windows, especially at night with the lights on. Scrapers, paintbrushes, screwdrivers, and pliers left on the floor can evoke *Task B.S.*, while electrical devices, such as power drills and lamps, can trigger *Wired-Up B.S.* A stepladder might look like a gallows or guillotine, and this impression can be heightened by the harsh lighting and lack of normal amenities. Decorating also forces you to inspect things closely and become intimately acquainted with the fabric of the building (see *Detail B.S.*).

In fact, renovating a room can be so B.S. that it is tempting to prolong the work indefinitely. Whenever there is a need to loosen your bowels, simply wander around the unfortunate chamber and inspect the items of work left undone. This is a deliciously perverse thing to do, like picking at a sore to prevent it healing.

And then, there are attics—empty and desolate spaces, with bare floorboards, dust, and old, forgotten toys. And abandoned furniture.

Empty Building B.S.

Buildings designed for large numbers of people seem unnaturally empty when the crowds have left. Their echoing corridors, cavernous rooms, and disused equipment ache with loneliness. Someone entering such a place can feel the very walls chide them to leave—as if the building is haunted by the absence of people. This feeling is similar to the one after an accustomed sound stops.

The response to an empty building can come from a heightened sense of separation, rather like the bowel-wrenching moment of missing a boat or train. Leaving the flock is courting disaster, and empty buildings seem to elicit this primitive fear (see *Separation from the Herd B.S.*). In fact, something similar to *Empty Building B.S.* occurs whenever we act alone (see *Egregious B.S.*). Compounding the anxiety is the suspicion that the crowd has left for a very good reason. Perhaps they evacuated because a predator stalked them. Or worse still, they were taken…

Empty Building B.S. also relies on the contrast between the quiet present and the busy past—a bowel-troubling nostalgia for when the building was bustling with activity. Three categories emerge, according to the time that has elapsed since the building became quiet: temporarily closed, recently disused, and disused for a long period:

i. temporarily closed. Public buildings and workplaces that are closed for the night, weekend, or a holiday are very B.S. Examples include: an old town library after the librarian has locked up for the night, a technical college after the students have left for the day, a railway station waiting room after the last train has gone, offices after business hours, and garages that are shut (but which you can peer into and see the vehicles in for repair).

ii. recently disused. Industrial buildings, such as factories or warehouses, are B.S., especially if some machinery remains as a reminder of the work once carried out there (see *Task B.S.*). Such places are frequently broken into and it is possible that the B.S. is a motive behind some of these events (see *Crime B.S.*). There is a strong sense that their users have fled.

iii. disused for a long period. Ancient monuments, ruins, and the like are extreme forms of disused buildings and create their own distinctive flavour of B.S. Wandering around ruins that are exposed to the elements can be nearly unbearable. The greater the sense of history, the more the past resonates through the structure, and the sharper is the contrast with the quiet present. If high-tech equipment is introduced into the scene, making the building appear even more ancient by comparison, then the effect is magnified. Such a mixture can occur in surveying, archaeological, or forensic work. Psychic research may also require sensitive equipment to be positioned in old buildings. This juxtaposition of modern equipment and old structures can generate a very potent mixture of *Empty Building B.S.* and *Wired-Up B.S.* Derelict industrial buildings, especially those associated with old technologies, are strongly bowel stirring. Examples include windmills and houses by canals.

The sequence of occupation, disuse, and occupation is the temporal equivalent of two houses separated by exposed territory. *Festival B.S.* discusses this notion of empty and crowded time.

Privacy, being a prerequisite for an easy bowel motion, plays a role in *Empty Building B.S.*, since buildings that emphasise emptiness give a deep sense of privacy. This creates a terrible confusion over whether the interior building is a refuge or a hostile space. The privacy suggests that the interior is a potential toilet, but the absence of other people suggests something is wrong with the place. Indeed, a central theme of *Empty Building B.S.* is the urge to find a hiding place within the building or to quit the building altogether (see also *Embedded Building B.S.* or *House within a House B.S.*). Empty buildings give the impression that they might harbour other beings—creatures that do not live like us and have different ideas about comfort—creatures that might prefer their homes to be cold, and dark, and quiet.

When in a comfortable and private situation, contemplating an empty building from afar generates a pure and powerful B.S. Many fantasies employ an empty building, but provide a device that offers some measure of safety. Examples include the flying pogo stick in the deserted shopping mall, and the comfortable armchair—complete with floral design—on the third floor of a disused clothing factory. Deserted hangars, factories, underground car parks, and warehouses often feature in films when there is a need to create a bowel-throbbing anticipation of danger.

By extension, *Empty Building B.S.* becomes *Empty City B.S.* and then *Empty World B.S.*

Empty City B.S.

Ghost towns can elicit this B.S. Deserted mining towns that were built and flourished during the gold rush are especially good for evoking this feeling. The strong emotions associated with gold fever leave these places with an air of past trauma and struggle. It can be discomforting to wander around them, rather like visiting the scene of a disaster. However, this feeling is quite subtle, since the buildings may all be in excellent condition—especially if the town has been restored. It seems irrational to be frightened of an interesting historical site, but our guts are still agitated. We sense danger and suspect that something is watching us.

It seems that the unconscious mind, being unused to deserted towns, has constructed what it sees as a satisfying explanation for the lack of people. It concludes, since the buildings are still intact, that the inhabitants were the victims of an unknown and extremely sophisticated predator.

This effect of a ghost town can be enhanced if the place has been reconstructed like a museum exhibit, with everyday objects still in their normal places (see *Museum B.S.*). A bicycle stands against a railing as if the rider had just stepped inside for a cup of tea. Cups and saucers are arranged on the kitchen table, clothes lie half folded in the bedroom, and the signs outside the shops creak eerily in the wind. The people must have left in a hurry, or were destroyed or captured, before they could tidy up or leave a warning. *Empty City B.S.* is the architectural equivalent of *Empty Vessel B.S.*, whose epitome is the *Mary Celeste*.

Empty World B.S.

The B.S. helps explain the attraction of science fiction that explores post-holocaust scenarios in which most of the population has been wiped out by a nuclear war or an infectious disease. The empty world scenario elicits *Primitive B.S.* as the survivor looks out onto a vast and exposed landscape. There is no one left to help defend against predators, and the remaining buildings offer an endless array of potential toilets, refuges, and traps. The survivor reverts to the ancestral opportunistic defaecator who first gazed across the open land. He prepares to venture into fresh territory as he contemplates an evolutionary leap. All sorts of pioneering adventures generate this *Pioneering B.S.*, which is related to *Egregious B.S.*

Deserted Public Spaces

Market squares, alleyways, and roads can generate the sense of an absent crowd in the same way that empty buildings do. They are very B.S. at night, when everyone else is asleep (see *Edge of the Herd B.S.*). If these spaces are deserted during the day, they suggest that a catastrophe has wiped out the population (see *Empty City B.S.* and *Empty World B.S.*), or that the population is expecting trouble, as in the main street of a Western town before a gunfight.

It can be very B.S. to walk the streets at night, especially after a rainstorm. The roads stretch out like glistening ribbons and traffic lights reflect off the wet surfaces. The continuing action of the lights, in the absence of any traffic, gives the scene a weird, robotic feel, suggesting that machines are still working long after the population has gone. This sense that machines will continue to operate after people have disappeared is exceedingly B.S. and often used in science fiction. This fear of being superseded by robots occurs because machines look like alien life-forms that have replaced humans. This is B.S. on a grand, species-threatening scale.

Change of Use B.S.

Buildings become B.S. when they are no longer used for their original purpose. Surrealistic changes of use, when unexpected objects or activities are set in a building, generate powerful B.S. feelings. A good example is the conversion of an old factory or warehouse into a fashionable living area, or a base for a particular project. Films frequently use this technique, with characters living in outrageous apartments inside industrial buildings. A secret or urgent project, possibly involving surveillance, may have its headquarters in a converted industrial or public building. The converse, when a dwelling is converted for industrial use, is also B.S. Such projects usually have electronic equipment strewn about, which generates *Wired-Up B.S.*

Change of Use B.S. is amplified by *Empty Building B.S.* when there has been a period of disuse between the original and current uses. Thus, a factory that is converted to a living area is more B.S. if it has lain empty for several years before conversion.

Embedded Building or House within a House B.S.

Buildings located inside larger buildings are very B.S. There is a *B.S. Cascade* at work, and an echo of the childhood construction of houses from cardboard boxes, cushions, and the like. Children will make shelters from almost anything and then hide in them. For them, the adult house is too big for comfort, and so they build a shelter at their own scale. A nested nest, as it were. This implies that *Embedded Building B.S.* works because the scale of the greater building seems suited to a larger and hence more threatening species. This urge to construct an embedded shelter, when the existing building is too large to be comforting, persists into adult life.

Shopping malls often have examples of embedded buildings. Malls are like enclosed streets and so their shops may emulate external ones in an attempt to recreate the intimate feel of an old-fashioned street. Booths may stand in the middle of large open spaces in the mall, offering information services or shoe repairs, key cutting, and engraving. Open-topped booths can be intolerably B.S.—as you will appreciate if you look down into them. This is best done from a nearby escalator, since this adds a nice touch of *Staircase B.S.*, but if one is not available, then try viewing the booth from the next storey of the mall. The exposed booth effect is heightened if the booth has finished trading for the night. The tools, till, telephone, and all the other requisites for the trade, are exposed to view and the booth looks like a dissected shop, with all its workings laid bare. It is also reminiscent of an abandoned ship adrift in the middle of the floor (see *Empty Vessel B.S.*).

Magazine huts or telephone boxes huddled beneath the arches of larger buildings are excruciating examples of embedded buildings.

The main reason for the attraction of an embedded building is its size and simplicity—for an enemy cannot easily hide inside it. The larger building, by contrast, could be swarming with predators. The small embedded building is rather like a loose-fitting suit of armour. The nested building might also give the impression of having once been a vehicle that somehow landed and then took root (see *Impeded Vehicle B.S.*).

An interesting extension to this idea is the inclusion in a large-scale structure of a small-scale model of that structure. For example, the captain of a ship might have a model of his vessel in his quarters. Similarly, a building might have its own original architectural model displayed in the foyer (see *Map B.S.* and *Model B.S.*).

Private Spaces Dissolved in Public Ones

The juxtaposition of private and public spaces is very B.S. Gardens next to roads—or gardens with public rights of way crossing them—are good examples, but the effect is stronger when the interiors of private and public buildings are combined. An obvious example is the open-plan office, where the private zone is barely demarcated from the common area (see also *Task B.S.*). It is possible to imagine a more extreme form of this admixture by dissolving a private building or room into a public one. The public building digests the private one and incorporates its components into its dilated body. Bookshelves, chairs, and television stands are swept outwards by the process, creating a shipwreck of a private room cast onto a public beach.

Imagine a small, cosy, book-lined study that had been penetrated by a public library and forced to expand hundreds of times to accommodate it. Personal shelves are thrown to the far corners of the new space, and the modest collection of well-tended books is diluted by thousands of volumes of dog-eared library books. An expanded version of this appears in the *Fantasies* section, under *Owning Bookshelves in the Local Library*. *Dissolved Building B.S.* is an extreme version of *Embedded Building B.S.* since the inner structure is dispersed. An embedded building remains intact as an identifiable bolt-hole, whereas a dissolved one is hard to detect and offers no sanctuary—it becomes a diffuse, virtual refuge. An exploded, embedded building. It is as if the private room had crash-landed into the public one, and its wreckage strewn everywhere.

One root of *Dissolved Building B.S.* may be the sense that the private room has been eaten and its semi-digested remnants scattered.

A less intense version of mixing private and public occurs in stately homes that open to the public while they are still lived in. Similarly, a guest house whose owners still live there, or a private house that accommodates a tea room, can be bowel stirring. In these latter cases, a private toilet may well have to double as a public one.

Contrasting Building B.S.

Very different buildings standing shoulder to shoulder can create this type of B.S., especially when old structures sit beside modern ones, or industrial buildings loom next to small dwellings. Examples include a church that survived redevelopment and ended up surrounded by high-rise office blocks—the decorative masonry of the church reflected in the new glassy buildings—and a cottage built in the middle of an industrial estate. In this disturbed placement, the cottage's picket fence, rose garden, and lace curtains look deeply out of place next to the warehouses and builders' supply yards.

Buildings

SOME PARTS OF BUILDINGS ARE B.S. in their own right and can be even more disturbing when isolated. For example, a door and its frame standing alone in a field, or a window propped against the ticket office of a busy underground railway station. Some elements seem designed or decorated for the B.S., whether or not they are set in a building. Perhaps they were put in on purpose, but it seems more likely they succeeded because they appealed to clients or residents, and neither the architect nor the occupier was aware of the mechanism—an unconscious selection has taken place, in which B.S. buildings or designs survived because of unrecognised feelings. This echoes popular film and television productions that have B.S. elements. Some of these structures are listed below.

a) Doors, Windows, and their Extensions
Doors, hatches, manhole covers, and the like are all B.S. because they allow the ingress of predators and enemies

(see *Portal B.S.*). Leaving a door unlocked or partly ajar can emphasise this, increasing the B.S. response. Doors tend to separate contrasting spaces and so door frames have a strong *B.S. Gradient* across them. Consequently, objects that straddle doorways, connecting the interior of the building with the outside and preventing the door from closing, are very B.S. (imagine sitting in a wooden chair in a doorway, with your back to the outside world). Portal-straddling things also generate *Partition Penetrating B.S.* It is very B.S. to hover in doorways. A vertical version would be to sit on a chair that projected halfway above a manhole cover in the middle of the road. If the chair could be raised and lowered mechanically, so much the better.

Porches and awnings project into the street and increase the B.S. of doors. A hotel might have a tent-like extension that shelters guests on the walk from their cars to the lobby. The discomfort is increased by the knowledge that the roof extends over a public footpath. On a more modest scale, some houses have porches that offer protection from the elements for a person fumbling for a key. Porches are even more B.S. if they open straight onto the street, rather than into a garden, because of the enhanced *Proximity to Traffic B.S.*

Arcades that run along the sides of buildings create a space that is half inside and half outside. Shops may have windows that look out into arcades. It can be uncomfortable to window shop along these arcades, even though they provide some shelter from bad weather.

There is a sense that the building is reaching out to embrace and protect those in the street. These intermediate spaces sometimes contain small roofed shelters such as magazine stalls, which provoke a version of *Embedded Building B.S.*

Bay windows project beyond the main outline of a building and can extend a comfortable living room (or office) smoothly into the street. This gives a person who is safely inside a taste of the hostile exterior. Bay windows are more B.S. at ground level when there is no front garden to separate them from the street and those who walk down it.

Balconies are B.S. because they project into space, beyond the building. A person on a balcony is exposed to view and to the elements. However, the sanctuary of the building is immediately behind, and this creates a steep *B.S. Gradient*. Balconies that are close to the ground are more accessible to passers-by and so are more distressing than those on upper storeys. Balconies that jut from the corner of a building are more B.S. than those in the middle of a wall. This is because a corner balcony is exposed on two fronts, and there are two roads along which predators or enemies might travel. If a balcony looks out across a roundabout or other intersection, this feeling of exposure to several routes of attack is increased still further (see *Proximity to Traffic B.S.*).

Falling from a high balcony is more dangerous than falling from a low one, and the higher one goes, the more the B.S. is replaced by vertigo. To illustrate this, imagine having tea and cakes on a balcony that sits only a few feet above street level. There is virtually no danger of injury from an accidental fall, and yet the B.S. would be intolerable. Now imagine doing the same thing on a balcony that is 20 storeys high. You might admire the view, or be made giddy by the height, but the B.S. would be much weaker. You could finish your tea!

Balconies and bay windows may be the modern equivalent of primordial forest lookouts. On the ground, standing hidden behind an old tree, surely covered in creepers, with some undergrowth between him and the open ground, Early B.S. Man might have felt the same thing that a person today feels when looking out from a ground-floor bay window or balcony.

Balconies and bay windows sometimes look like buds from the main building. If this budding process were to continue, then the connection with the main building would diminish, and finally snap, throwing balconies and bay windows off as separate objects. The ultimate versions would be the balcony that evolved into something like a bird table with railings and a 360° free-standing bay window. Such constructions would be exquisitely B.S. Early B.S. Man would recognise them as lone trees in the middle of a plain. Balconies are more B.S. if they are supported on struts because of *Pole B.S.*

b) Separate Buildings

Garden sheds, sentry boxes (and their modern equivalents, such as the small shelters for car park attendants), external toilets, generator sheds, and the like are B.S. by virtue of being exposed, small, and associated with a bigger building. Used sparingly, objects that make them more homely and comfortable increase the effect. These could include a low-wattage free-standing heater, a wooden chair, a picture on the wall, and perhaps a few books on a shelf. It is best not to overdo these home comforts, or the separate structure will seem too much like the main building.

It may be that the urge of children to make tree houses is an expression of *Separate Structure B.S.* In due course, this might develop into a love of camping. Tents are B.S. because they are fragile and temporary. Separate structures echo the clumps of trees that dotted the primordial plain. They are the potential toilets that Early B.S. Man would have noted as he planned his hazardous route across the exposed landscape. External toilets are classic B.S. examples of separate structures. *Separate Structure B.S.* might also help to explain the phenomenal power of telephone boxes to agitate the belly.

c) Connecting Structures

Corridors, covered walkways, bridges linking two buildings, and all kinds of steps and stairs are examples of B.S. connecting structures. They are designed for transit, not dwelling. There is a feeling of mild exposure when travelling from one room or building to another, and so one hurries through as quickly as possible. Consequently, the B.S. effect can be heightened if there is some reason to tarry. If this reason is perverse or surreal, so much the better. For example, you might find yourself in a long and empty corridor and decide to make a telephone call from a handset on the floor.

Alternatively, you could be sitting at a small table about to be served cream tea. Unfortunately, the table is on the landing of a stairway that runs up the glass-sided corner of an office block. You might even be persuaded to tackle some paperwork that sits on a desk in an underground passage in a hospital. Taken to extremes, this idea leads to the temptation to establish an office in a corridor.

The two places joined by a connecting structure become a starting point and a destination. In this relationship they are compared, and the contrast generates the B.S. The connecting structure acts like a wire spanning a voltage drop, except that here it is a *B.S. Gradient* rather than an electrical one (see also *Partition Penetrating Devices*). As a child, I vividly remember the sensation of leaving a warm and crowded sitting room at Christmas and venturing along the cold and dark passage to the toilet or kitchen. There was always the temptation to stop and look into the other rooms because of the delicious sense of desolation these places had in contrast to the party (see *Disappointed Structure B.S.*). If my trip involved going up the stairs, all the better (see below and *Festival B.S.*).

d) Stairs, Escalators, and Lifts

Stairs, and their motorised counterparts, escalators and lifts, are potently B.S., since they connect different levels of a building. The higher storeys seem more secure than the lower ones, perhaps because of an ancient association of safety with height. *Staircase B.S.* may therefore derive from memories of climbing trees to find refuge. The more closely the stairs resemble trees, the stronger the effect. Steeper stairs are better, since tree trunks tend to be steep (and if they were not, then predators could easily follow). Balustrades suggest an open lattice-work of branches (see *Skeletal B.S.*) or a line of slim tree trunks. Sitting on the stairs and peering through the balustrade gives us the atavistic thrill of feeling like an ape watching from its leafy refuge. Ropes and rope ladders hanging from a hatch in the roof may mimic creepers hanging from branches, while spiral staircases might suggest a tree trunk. Neat though this picture is, it is complicated by childhood memories of playing on the stairs, or of creeping down them after being sent to bed.

Escalators are like staircases with engines, and so provoke *Motorised B.S.* Ancient ones with wooden slats are more like conventional timber stairs, and so the effect is stronger. The very long escalators that ferry people to and from underground railway stations are very B.S. (in

fact, everything about the underground railway is B.S.—
see *Going Underground B.S.*). An escalator is really a motorised escape route, a sort of fixed vehicle (see *Impeded
Vehicle B.S.* and *Rail B.S.*).

Lifts are interior vehicles that create *Indoor Vehicle B.S.*
They also move along definite paths, which triggers *Rail
B.S.* Although most lifts are little enclosed rooms, some
have glass walls. These delightful objects can run inside
the building, giving giddy views of the atrium, or run
outside, giving panoramas of the city. Others are more
like cages. Some contain an emergency phone, which
adds a nice touch of *Telecommunications B.S.* The handset is usually nested in a wall cabinet, which does not
help matters.

Lift shafts rise vertically through floors as *Partition Penetrating Devices*. Being dark and concealed from normal
view, they provoke *Secret Passage B.S.*, while the heavy-
duty chains and cables trigger *Wired-Up B.S.* and *External
Mechanism B.S.* Some lift shafts are openwork mesh
structures, and when their lifts are also mesh, the effect
is of a cage travelling within a cage.

A conventional lift is like a vertical underground train. It
moves through dark tunnels, and when it emerges at a
stop, where everything is brightly lit, the doors open automatically and people get on and off. The automatic
opening of lift doors can be quite threatening because
the occupant is exposed to whatever dangers exist on
that floor. The safe little cubicle becomes a trap (see

Refuge-Trap B.S.). The movement of a lift can be very B.S. because it seems slightly beyond our control. This type of B.S. is common to all vehicles that cannot easily be steered or stopped, or which behave capriciously, or can be controlled by others, or whose doors open automatically. This quality is exploited in films when a lift conveys its hapless occupant towards danger (usually a psychopath waiting on a lower floor). The victim might struggle to override the instructions being sent to the lift by the other party, but the lift moves inexorably towards danger. In this sense, the lift is like a mechanical feeding organ that conveys prey to the waiting mouth.

Some very old lifts in fancy department stores or in public buildings even have an operator, who sits on a small wooden chair and spends the day going from floor to floor, like a tram driver trapped in an interior route. Operator-controlled lifts may have framed pictures on the walls, and furniture and other items that make the lift like a small sitting room or office. Seeing such an arrangement may lead you to consider renting part of a busy lift for your own office. A filing cabinet, small desk, desk lamp, and a fax machine could hem you into one corner and separate you from the flux of passengers. A free-standing coat and umbrella stand, positioned on one of the floors that the lift visited, would complete the effect.

Because lifts are like house-bound vehicles, you cannot help but feel slightly sorry for them in the same way that you might feel sympathetic for a window that has a very poor outlook, or a train in a museum that only has a short length of track (see *Disappointed Structure B.S.*). The thought that a lift might break free from its shaft and trundle down the high street is quite compelling. Fantasies of releasing benighted structures—and watching their adventures—create *Liberation B.S.*

e) Secret Passages & Rooms

Secret passages and secret rooms are very B.S. because they offer concealment as well as physical protection. The delicious sense of hiding from the world gives them a special B.S. frisson. This thrill is akin to the infantile delight of playing hide-and-seek, and strongly suggests a childhood origin for this type of B.S. Children like hiding behind furniture or in cupboards and are always looking for nooks and crannies to squeeze into. A hankering for secret places and concealed doors that open into them persists into adulthood. This desire may be catered for in science fiction, horror, and spy films that feature elaborate establishments hidden inside or under apparently normal buildings. Revolving bookcases, chairs that drop through floors, panels that open in walls, and strange external entranceways are all used to gain access to these places. This use of furniture as a portal to another world is a common device, and the evocative power of furniture is discussed below. Having the secret space at a different level adds elements of *Going Underground B.S.* and *Staircase B.S.*

The hidden place is usually a centre of illicit activity, recalling the naughtiness of hidden children. In science fiction or espionage stories, the activity may be highly sophisticated and utilise futuristic or alien technologies or supernatural methods. Developing advanced weapons of mass destruction, building spaceships, or reanimating corpses may be done in these subterranean super facilities. This covert use of advanced, or even magical, techniques strongly suggests the rich imagination of a child secreted away in a corner of the house or garden. Perhaps constructing these objects or performing these feats of technology or magic in hidden places also recalls the gestation and rearing of young in protected burrows. In other words, when we respond to these images, it is because we recognise, at some dim level, the biological imperative to hide away in a safe place and produce babies. Conversely, the secret place that we stumble upon may be the burrow of a predator. This seems a plausible explanation of why we find the image of an evil genius building underground horrors so compelling. We see, in symbolic form, a super predator rearing its brood. The dual role of the secret place as our own home or the nest of a predator is an example of a *B.S. Paradox*.

In fantasy fiction, the entrance may be to another universe, often with a different set of natural laws that permit fabulous plots to unfold. There may even be a succession of embedded universes dwelling behind the camouflaged doorway.

Secret places might have peepholes looking out to the exterior or into other rooms. This means that the concealed person can watch without being seen, and recalls the B.S. of invisibility. The highly illicit nature of this type of voyeurism elicits a brand of *Trespass B.S.* in which the fear of discovery is almost titillating.

Secret passages may run, warren-like, throughout a building, allowing someone to move around everywhere without attracting attention. Many films use air-conditioning conduits in this capacity. These covert routes may echo the routes that link potential toilets together, and they may even recall ancient memories of safe highways in the forest canopy.

Secret passages might connect different buildings together or connect a building to a distant and secret entrance. Such secret routes might be used to escape persecution, to allow sexual access to a forbidden population, or to pursue an illegal trade. Smugglers' tunnels running from an underground cellar to the sea are a perfect example of the latter. These places are doubly B.S. because they housed an activity that took a reasonable amount of time to perform (and was usually illicit). This is akin to the increased B.S. in corridors supplied with an excuse to tarry (see *Connecting Structures* above). It is generally the case that performing a complex task while in a state of real or potential exposure is highly bowel stirring (see *Task B.S.*).

In some cases, hidden passages can conceal invaders, and the passages are like vessels in a body down which a parasite travels. Psychopaths or alien life forms might watch their human prey through the slats of an airway and scuttle off down the conduits before they can be caught.

f) Exposed Supply Lines & Meters

Water pipes, sewage pipes, and gas pipes are normally concealed. When they are exposed to view—the architectural equivalent of having one's guts on the outside—they are very B.S. Some famous buildings emphasise their structural supports, as well as their supply lines, by having them exposed to view. They have made an aesthetic virtue out of functional necessities—though some of these features may be decorations masquerading as functional elements. There was a fashion several years ago to make a design feature from water and sewage pipes. Many private homes of the era are still bedecked with ugly pipes that are impossible to hide or beautify.

Meters for gas, water, and electricity are all exceedingly B.S. They are often squat and vaguely robotic, with their dials and pipes. These useful mechanical devices sit patiently monitoring flows day and night, rain or shine, but they are often relegated to the most horrendously bowel-tumbling locations, such as in cellars, under archways, in porches, or even in purpose-built shelters.

Water meters can sit ticking away in little bunkers amid the roses of a front garden. Some old terraced houses have arched tunnels between them that give access to the back gardens, and these external corridors might contain meters or electricity junction boxes and be strewn with wires and pipes. A passageway strung with cables looks like a very dubious route. There is the suspicion that it is really a trap (see *Refuge-Trap B.S.* and *Wired-Up B.S.*). The unfortunate placement of these cables and instruments can also trigger *Disappointed Structure B.S.*, especially if the walls are damp and covered with moss, while their utilitarian appearance can elicit *Primitive Machine B.S.* Huge banks of meters, such as occur in power stations or pump houses, are disturbing too, perhaps because of *Probe B.S.* (control rooms also trigger *Lightning Conductor B.S.* and *Remote Control B.S.*).

In some modern buildings, the supply lines are neatly hidden away. They may travel underground, pass along conduits, and remain modestly concealed behind panels. In others, a point is made of exposing air-conditioning pipes and other functional items that are normally concealed in the ceiling. This can give the interior the appearance of having been partly dissected. When such supplies are added to an existing structure, there may be little attempt to conceal them, and this can generate *Wired-Up B.S.*

Telephone and electricity supplies are often carried by overhead wires which travel down streets, hang across gardens and enter houses via strange connectors. The poles that carry them often have mysterious little boxes and other attachments screwed to them. Such supply lines seem vulnerable to attack, for someone could easily snip the telephone cables or cut the electricity wires (see *External Mechanism B.S.*).

WALLS, FLOORS, ROOFS AND OTHER PARTITIONS

Walls

Internal walls separate rooms from one another, while external walls separate the inside of a building from the outside. Consequently, walls have huge *B.S. Gradients* across them. A hole in a wall can churn the guts because it links two different spaces and provides an ingress for enemies or predators. Straddling the hole, one is torn by the *B.S. Gradient,* and there is a powerful urge to enter one space or the other to resolve the tension. Sitting in the hole makes this movement more difficult, and so a chair placed across the hole, with two legs in one room and two in another, is an awful place to sit. A complex version of this is *The Toilet that Straddles an External Wall* in the Fantasies section.

Floors

Floors separate one storey from another. They are usually covered by carpets, tiles, or linoleum. Adults rarely get down on their hands and knees to inspect these floor coverings, but to very young children they are fascinating landscapes. Dead insects, pieces of fluff that roll around like tumbleweed, scraps of paper and other jetsam populate this land. The child may be able to lift the edge of the carpet and glimpse the floorboards underneath. This is normal curiosity in children, but when an adult does it, it can be very B.S. An adult can go further and lift the floorboards to reveal the space between the joists. Usually, this is done to lay wiring or plumbing, but it could be done purely as a B.S. exercise. This space inside the floor is often a graveyard of ephemera, and removing the floorboards can feel like opening an archaeological site.

Frequently, old newspapers are discovered buried there. Quite why people should feel compelled to hide newspapers under floorboards is something of a mystery, but it seems to be a rather common practice (in fact, this may be one of the proofs of the ubiquity of the B.S.). Cigarette packets, tickets, instruction leaflets, small pieces of wood and piping, screws and other items are often found there too. Sometimes, they have lain undisturbed and unsuspected for decades. They are like little encapsulations of the time when the floorboards were last lifted. Perhaps they were dropped during a coffee break that was taken seventeen years ago. Occasionally, the dates can be verified by the newspaper remnants. These assemblages underfoot may have survived years of rough and tumble above them—countless carpet cleanings, footsteps and even several changes of carpet have left them in peace. Compare this to the fate of objects at the surface, either blowing free across the exposed boards, or lodged in the pile of a carpet. These small things can be removed whenever the carpet is vacuumed or they can be shifted by the slightest breeze.

Objects *on* the floor and objects *in* the floor are both B.S., but for different reasons. Those on the surface are B.S. because they recall childhood inspection of the world at ground level, and because they are so unstable as arrangements. Those in the floor, beneath the floorboards, are B.S. because they are so stable and lie in a space that is undisturbed compared with the heavily trafficked and frequently swept space immediately above (like objects in a museum that stands next to a busy street). The space beneath floorboards is a secret room. It is also comparable to those time capsules that are filled with examples of current art and then sealed up in the hope that they will be opened by future generations. Such objects are rather like unmanned time machines (see *Emissary Machines*).

Roofs

A roof shelters a building from the weather. There is a strong contrast between the outer surface, which might be pelted with rain and exposed to freezing temperatures and high winds, and the inside, which is dry, warm and still. A roof might symbolise armour. This is more obvious with a tiled roof because the slates are reminiscent of scales. The rafters form a rib cage against the felt or slates, giving the vault the look of the inside of a tortoise's carapace. The building becomes a living organism, hunched against the elements.

There is frequently a cavity, the roof space or attic, which accommodates such B.S. things as water tanks, discarded toys and old tools. Some roof spaces are converted into offices or bedrooms, but most are not proper rooms at all, and one has the urge to run out of them into the sunlight or return to a more comfortable room downstairs. Such rarely visited attics give the impression that time has stopped. It can be extremely B.S. to stand on a stepladder and look through the hatch into the roof space. The lower half of your body is near the ceiling of the hallway or bedroom, and your torso and head are in the roof space. This leaves your viscera spanning two very different spaces, which is very B.S. (see *Partition Penetrating Devices* below). Additionally, you are near the ceiling (B.S.) and near the floor of the roof space (B.S.). A roof space can also be like a secret room. Imagine how bowel stirring it would be to move around among the rafters and spy on people below through peepholes set in the ceiling.

Miscellaneous Partitions

Internal partitions, especially those used to separate work areas in open-plan offices, are B.S. because they only weakly delimit safe personal territory from the territories of other people and from common areas and thoroughfares. Old wooden partitions, with windows made from frosted glass, are more B.S. than modern ones. They can be found in some old offices and hospitals.

Partition Penetrating Devices

Because partitions are the sites of strong *B.S. Gradients*, structures that penetrate them—and so link two disparate spaces—are very B.S. They are comparable to wires that connect two regions of different voltage. Examples include laundry chutes, chimneys, lift shafts, and communication tubes on ships.

Periscopes let you spy on a territory (or a surface of water) without exposing yourself and risking attack (see *Probe B.S.*). A periscope looking into the attic above or the cellar below would be an exquisitely B.S. device. If the other room were dark, then the periscope would need lights, making matters worse. An optical device (like a *camera obscura*) that poked through the roof, enabling you to look out onto the world at roof height, would be very B.S. for the same reason—more so if it were remotely controlled.

A series of looking devices, scattered around a building, can be imagined. These could be much simpler than periscopes, perhaps nothing more than peepholes. Because they allow you to look without being seen, they are stirring—more so if they peer out from a secret room or passage (see also *Secret Passages & Rooms* above). Security officers may sit at consoles and watch multiple television sets that monitor scattered rooms in large buildings. This exceedingly bowel-throbbing image occurs commonly in films.

Pneumatically powered delivery systems that once served offices are excruciatingly B.S. They had chutes down which small canisters carried office memos and the like. The tubes snaked around and penetrated floors, connecting the various offices like a partly dissected underground railway system.

Model railways serve a similar function. They might transport food around a restaurant, or goods and paperwork around an office, their little locomotives chugging through tunnels cut in walls. Such systems generate *Rail B.S.* because the chutes or rails make the routes explicit and permanent. There are also elements of *Wired-Up B.S.* Whether as tools or toys, train sets are like miniature public transport systems, so they generate a version of *Model B.S.* and *Travelling B.S.* by proxy.

FITMENTS

Fireplaces

Fireplaces are B.S. because they are a source of warmth and security; they are the focus of attention and the very heart of a house. Huge fireplaces, like those in stately homes, castles, and some pubs, suggest a room within a room and so generate *Embedded Building B.S.*

Fire may have warded off predators in prehistoric times, which could explain why we find external fireplaces so B.S. today. Exposed grates and chimneys can be found in the ruins of old cottages. As the strongest part, the chimney often remains after the rest of the house has collapsed. These structures can exert an ancient pull on the modern bowel as they stand alone and defiant, surrounded by rubble and wild grass. Brick and concrete gas-powered barbecues are bowel stirring too, especially if the weather is cold and forbidding, and the barbecues are located far from dwellings (an external cooker is rather like an external chimney or a piece of furniture that is left out of doors). An external fireplace can give the impression of a house without walls. The state of exposure that this implies is very bowel-churning.

Demolition can also expose fireplaces and make them external. When terraces of houses are being knocked down, fireplaces can have a brief but glorious period under the sky (see *Dissection B.S.*). Those at ground level are bad enough, but the ones on upper storeys are excruciating. Many years ago they might have warmed a bedroom, but now they hang aloft on a temporary external wall, perhaps still framed by scraps of floral wallpaper. Imagine jacking yourself up in a mechanical chair and reaching out to dust the mantlepiece.

Chimneys are also B.S. because they penetrate the fabric of a house (see *Partition Penetrating Devices*). Those that lie at one end of a detached house and form a prominent feature are B.S. because they straddle the external wall and stand half in the garden. Some chimneys generate a mild *False Vehicle B.S.* because they make the building to which they are attached vaguely reminiscent of a steam locomotive.

Bathroom Fitments

Bathroom fitments with exposed supports and plumbing are often B.S. Examples include a sink held up by brackets with its waste pipe in view, a claw-footed bath standing in the middle of a large bathroom, and an old gas water heater above a bath. All bathroom fitments are more bowel stirring when out of doors (especially if plumbed in). A bath that is placed outside a bathroom can generate an extreme version of *Sitting B.S.* Imagine bathing in a claw-footed bath in the middle of a deserted factory.

FURNITURE

Much of the B.S. importance of furniture is due to its association with interiors, which are generally places of refuge. Indeed, items of furniture can themselves represent refuges (see *False Refuge B.S.*). This is especially true of box-like items with doors. Some of this association may hark back to the childish delight in hiding in wardrobes and exploring cupboards (see *Embedded Building B.S.*). Other pieces, such as tables, may offer refuge simply because they are clear of the floor, where dangers may lurk (see *Pole B.S.*).

Because of the strong link between furniture and interiors, placing it out of doors can be highly unsettling. Enclosing walls are conspicuous by their absence, and this creates a heightened sense of exposure. In other words, these pieces draw your attention to the fact that you are not in a room. Not only that, but their scale is fitted to small interiors, and this makes the external space seem even larger. Similarly, even when they are indoors, most furniture is placed against walls, and so items that stand clear of walls look adrift and vulnerable. In both of these cases—out of doors and in the middle of floors—pieces of furniture make the surrounding space seem even more public and dangerous.

Certain abnormal arrangements can be unsettling because they suggest an agency has meddled with the accepted layout. Nonsensical or surrealistic placements hint at the presence of madness (a psychopath in the vicinity), or of a different kind of intelligence (a predator with alien thought processes). Very minor rearrangements could elicit a fear that someone has trespassed and not quite covered their tracks.

Furniture and Mobility

Unlike fixtures and fittings, furniture is mobile and can follow its owners when they move house or office. A piece of furniture could stay with a family for generations, travelling with them from house to house and even from one side of the world to the other. Such pieces may well outlast the buildings in which they spent so many years, and outlive their original buyers. Old pieces of furniture can provoke a powerful nostalgic twinge in the gut because they have witnessed so much. They are stalwart things in the changing lives of those around them.

Displaced Furniture

Furniture shifted from its normal position can be very B.S. Dragging an office desk into a foyer, taking a dresser from the breakfast room to the cellar, or removing a four-poster bed from its bedroom would have this effect. Consequently, moving house can be very challenging. Sitting on a tea chest, watching your settee, dining table, and bookcase being carted out can be nearly unbearable, especially if you are drinking coffee at the time (see *Feeding B.S.*). As the items wait in the street to be loaded into the removals van, they seem lost and forlorn (see *Out-of-Scale Furniture*, below). Seeing your possessions making their own way to the new house is seriously bowel tugging (see *In Transit in Parallel B.S.*).

Furniture that is elevated or sunken can be distressing. Imagine an office desk stuck on a pole, a settee hung from chains, a bureau sitting in a shallow trench, or a wardrobe at the bottom of a well. These images suggest the aftermath of a flood or earthquake.

Moving furniture out of doors can create surreal and B.S. tableaux. Having dinner in the middle of a public park at sunset, seated at an oak dining table with six formal chairs and a Welsh dresser (complete with ornaments and framed photographs), for example, would be excruciating. There was a fashion for things like this in the 1960s and 1970s, which suggests that psychotropic drugs can unleash bursts of B.S. creativity (see *Drug B.S.*). The B.S. might explain the urge to arrange someone's furniture out of doors as a prank.

Furniture in Contrast with its Surroundings

Furniture that contrasts strongly with its surroundings is very B.S. Heavy wooden furniture inside a tent is an extreme example. A less drastic, but still very effective, arrangement would be to fill a cheap rental property with high quality furniture. This would give the impression of a temporary occupation, even if it were maintained for years (someone who could afford such furnishings would obviously be slumming). Tensions might also arise because the furniture seems to have a greater solidity or longevity than the structure of the building (see *Temporary Structure B.S.*). The arrangement of furniture might even seem to belong to another building, which creates a sense of displacement. Installing expensive equipment can create a similar feeling (see *Wired-Up B.S.*). Running a business from such quarters generates the B.S. continuously, the strength of the business and its furnishings contrasting with the frailty of the house. There is the feeling of sailing under false colours, of concealing power in a humble building. These arrangements recall camouflage and mimicry (see *Hidden Power B.S.*).

Out-of-Scale Furniture

Most furniture is suited to a particular size of room. In a wrongly-sized room, a piece can be very B.S. Perhaps this is why reception desks in hotel foyers are so discomforting.

Furniture designed for a standard office or lounge room can look seriously out of place in an industrial space or showroom. In warehouses, especially those dealing with second-hand office furniture, the desks, bookcases, computer tables, and cabinets look like disoriented passengers milling around a ferry terminal. Knowing they are in transit excites a furniture version of *Travelling B.S.*

Bookcases

These are B.S. because they house books—relatively fragile objects that seem to have a personality. Books with personal significance, like old school texts or novels enjoyed during adolescence, amplify this effect.

Bookcases that look almost big enough to climb into may elicit *False Refuge B.S.* High shelves that keep things out of reach may suggest safety and also trigger childhood memories of climbing furniture to reach forbidden things.

Bookcases in unusual places are horrifically B.S. Imagine a small lockable model attached at knee height in somebody else's bathroom, a free-standing wooden one in the middle of a busy railway platform, or a bookcase in a boat (with a bar to prevent the books from falling out). Owning a remote bookcase is worrisome because other people may walk off with your books.

Chairs

Chairs symbolise sitting—a state where vigilance and escape are more difficult (see *Sitting B.S.*). This sitting-target effect can make a chair more like a trap than a refuge (*False Refuge B.S.*). Hovering or flying chairs are extremely colon-tugging, since they expose you to danger but offer the prospect of escape. Chairs are important in B.S. fantasies because of their intrinsic comfort, because of *Sitting B.S.,* and because they are usually displaced from their normal location. Many places can be made B.S. simply by installing a chair.

Most chairs are comfortable and so create a tension with their less comfortable surroundings. This is heightened in those with arms or wings that enclose the sitter and offer a sense of security. A soft enveloping chair is like a big protective animal that you can cuddle into and hide. From the back, it can be difficult to tell whether anyone is sitting in such a chair. More formal chairs, or those that are simply uncomfortable, can be gut-throbbing in a different way. They force an upright posture, creating feelings of subordination and vulnerability. Spindly wooden or metal chairs, with open frame structures, offer no sense of security and are more like cages that exhibit the sitter (see *Skeletal B.S.*).

For reasons of contrast, as well as exposure to danger, the location of a chair greatly influences its level of B.S. This explains why an over-stuffed armchair is far more B.S. when it stands on bare floorboards in an attic than when it sinks into deep-pile carpet in a lounge. Similarly, chairs in precarious locations are more B.S. than those in safe and conventional settings. Imagine suspending a chair from a wire so that it hangs just clear of the white lines in the middle of a road at night, or swings inches above the oily water of an urban canal.

Elevated chairs can be excruciating to contemplate or occupy. Real examples of such chairs can be seen at the side of some swimming pools or on certain beaches, where they are designed to give lifeguards a good view. However, it is more amusing to imagine conventional chairs elevated by improbable means. An office chair swaying on the top of a pole in a car park, an armchair bolted to the end of a mechanical arm, or a wickerwork settee slung from a crane in the middle of a demolition site, would be highly distressing. Similarly, an armchair bolted to an external brick wall four feet above a flower bed in someone else's garden would be a potent object. *Elevated Chair B.S.* is probably a compound of *Pole B.S.*, *Tower B.S.*, and *Sitting B.S.* However, *Childhood Perspective B.S.* might play its part, since such raised seats could be reminiscent of oversized high chairs. Any chair that is displaced from its standard location on the floor is disturbing because it is more difficult or dangerous to get out of. Thus, sunken chairs are highly bowel stirring too. A comfortable chair at the foot of the cellar steps would be deliciously difficult to sit in.

Chairs sometimes stand in the upstairs corridors of hotels. It is difficult to understand why anyone would use these chairs, except to B.S. themselves before checking out. It is delightful to imagine two such chairs positioned on either side of a corner, whose occupants converse using two tin cans and a stretched string. An elaborate exercise in *Turnabout B.S.* could use several chairs in a remote hotel. Each chair would be hidden from the others. A group of like-minded people could then arrange to sit in these chairs at a particular time on a particular day, but avoid all contact with each other. They could reconvene several weeks later in another town and compare notes.

Desks

Desks are B.S. because they suggest sitting (*Sitting B.S.*) and working (*Task B.S.*), which makes their positioning critical. Finding one at the foot of the cellar steps, or beside a swimming pool at night, would be quite unnerving. Temporarily placed desks are unsettling too. This can happen when a village hall is used to collect votes, when a school acts as a temporary police headquarters, or when a lecture theatre is used for student enrolment.

Desks in public thoroughfares or corridors are quite harrowing. Imagine the agonising B.S. of having your private desk block the upstairs walkway of a Victorian shopping arcade, or having it stand in the middle of an empty ground floor office. However, there are some choice examples in real life.

A hotel reception desk, moored at the far end of a dizzyingly huge foyer, always weakens my bowel. While registering, I can enjoy the prospect of passing several chairs, and perhaps a dresser, along the corridors leading to my room.

Airport check-in desks sit in the middle of vast public spaces. Hundreds of people with the *Travelling B.S.* come up to them each day and heave their luggage onto the built-in weighing machines. The bags are tagged and then carried off on conveyor belts to begin their journeys in parallel with their owners (see *In Transit in Parallel B.S.*). The constant throughput of humanity and its baggage tugs cruelly at the bowel.

Bureaus

Bureaus are more secure than desks because they have lockable covers. The work surface is enclosed and private, stacked with tiny drawers and compartments that are ideally suited for hiding papers, trinkets, and other oddments. An adult stashing things in a bureau may recall being a child, busily secreting little treasures around the house. The sense of enclosure, the feeling of years of work, and the storage of old and important documents all help to make bureaus B.S. A bureau is a stalwart thing, like a wooden safe. Standing quietly in the lounge room and harbouring the family's important records, it generates an oddly warm glow in the gut.

TERRITORY THAT SURROUNDS BUILDINGS

The territory that surrounds a building, and the things contained in it, are comparable to the open ground considered in *The Landscape of Potential Toilets*. This proximate landscape is rich with possibility.

Common Land

If the territory abutting a building is common ground, where anyone may pass, then the *B.S. Gradient* between the outside land and the inside of the building is huge. This is why buildings in the middle of public parks are so B.S. The front rooms and bay windows of terraced houses that meet the pavement are also disturbing for this reason.

Gardens

Gardens are tame little pieces of nature, intermediate between the tightly controlled internal environment and the wild. Most belong to an adjacent building, but some are remote, like allotments and distant gardens. The owner of a garden has a psychological advantage over most other people, since the average person will not trespass onto private property. Unfortunately, the real threats are from criminals, enemies, or predators who are unlikely to respect the boundaries. Consequently, open gardens are discomforting and B.S. They sit in the middle of a *B.S. Cascade*. The garden, with nothing to protect it but respect for property, sits physically and psychologically between the safety of the house and the uncertainty of the common land. The *B.S. Gradient*, from house to public land, becomes very steep when the adjacent garden is tiny.

Gardens might be reminiscent of ancient lookouts at the edge of the forest, especially if they abut a village green, a footpath, or a road. The owner can retreat into the building, much as his ancestor might have run for deeper cover in the trees.

A walled formal garden with statues and garden furniture can look like a room with the roof taken off.

Allotments and Distant Gardens

An allotment or far-away garden feels like a distant refuge. This is comforting if you are nearby and need a bolt-hole. At the same time, it is difficult to guard a distant plot. Dealing with remote territories generates *Remote Control B.S.* The most extreme version of a distant garden is an overseas colony that belongs to an empire (see *Outpost B.S.*).

An allotment, especially a rented one with little security of tenure, can provide hours of intense B.S. enjoyment. Growing vegetables that might be stolen creates a nice touch of *Task B.S.* A lock-up shed on an allotment is an intensely bowel-tugging refuge. A whole field of allotments, each with its own shed, is like a suburban rendering of *The Landscape of Potential Toilets*.

Imagine having to flee across allotments, hopping from one shed to another. Some sheds will be new and secure, while others will be tumbledown and easy to break into. Another B.S. exercise would be to install a telephone network to connect the sheds. You could sit in your wood and corrugated iron hovel and talk to the other gardeners. You would have created a field of ramshackle telephone boxes. These two thoughts can be combined into a bowel-wrecking fantasy in which you run from shed to shed, desperately trying to phone for help, while something pursues you across the ranks of Brussels sprouts, carrots, and cabbages.

Owning a small garden in a distant town is supremely B.S., especially if it is next to a public footpath. Ideally, the plot should be in front of someone else's house. Everyone assumes that the garden belongs to the house, and you derive great satisfaction from your secret ownership (see *Tending The Distant Garden* in the *Fantasies* section).

Garden Furniture

Garden tables and chairs are B.S., especially those in wood or stone. A park bench is disconcerting because it is a public seat in a public place (see *Sitting B.S.*). Bird tables, bird baths, statues, and other garden ornaments are effective, especially when covered in moss or lichen and located in dank and inaccessible parts of the garden.

B.S. BUILDINGS

Some types of buildings are exquisitely B.S. Industrial ones tend to be horrendously bowel stirring (*Task B.S.*), but aberrant dwellings and structures in unusual or precarious positions can be very disturbing too. The ultimate arrangement would be an external toilet poised at the edge of a cliff at the bottom of a sloping garden.

Lighthouses

Lighthouses teeter on the brink of land in isolated positions. They warn ships of danger, and so have an element of *Telecommunications B.S.* They are usually tall (*Tower B.S.*) with spiral stairs (*Staircase B.S.*) topped by a 360° bay window. External winches to lift things to the upper storeys, and other mechanisms, decorate their exteriors, generating *External Mechanism B.S.* They are most bowel wrenching on stormy nights when the contrast between their interior and the outside is fiercest.

Illuminated buoys anchored near shore are like floating lighthouses. Cut off from land, they are even more B.S. As small, tethered boats, they give a shudder of *Impeded Vehicle B.S.*

Observatories

Observatories gaze across the cosmos rather than the sea.

Optical telescopes are semi-enclosed instruments that generate *Telecommunications B.S.* The telescope, its supports, and the dome all turn slowly to track the stars. This coordinated movement of structures in a building generates a type of *Motorised B.S.* called *Rotating Building B.S.*

Observatories normally stand far from civilisation to avoid light pollution, and at high altitude to reduce atmospheric interference. Working on such isolated and expensive equipment triggers a potent *Task B.S.*

Radio telescopes generate the strongest form of *Telecommunications B.S.* imaginable. Those that scan the heavens for messages from aliens are the worst of all.

Mount Stromlo Observatory has an incredibly bowel-thumping arrangement. A short wooden spiral staircase rises from the library to the disused solar observatory. Staircases, especially wooden ones, create *Staircase B.S.*, and this one disappears into the roof space, making it a *Partition Penetrating Device*. The old observatory generates *Empty Building B.S.* When I sit in the corner of the library, leafing through back issues of science journals from around the world, I get into a real state.

A hobby observatory, located on the roof of a house, is a lookout and a *Partition Penetrating Device*. In addition— as a diminutive and domestic version of a large-scale piece of research equipment—it generates *Model B.S.*

Windmills

Windmills have *Rotating Building B.S.* because their top sections, containing the sails, rotate to face the wind. They also convert wind power into rotary movement and, by tapping into an elemental force, generate *Lightning Conductor B.S.*

Windmills usually stand isolated in flat areas, such as Holland or East Anglia. They are often associated with canals—the watery equivalent of railways—and so generate *Proximity to Water B.S.* and *Rail B.S.* This landscape contrasts strongly with the craggy environments favoured by lighthouses and observatories.

Windmills can be like galleons at sea, with their timbers creaking and their sails set against the wind. Nearby waterways and the undulations in the wheat fields add to the impression of the windmill as a land-bound ship. A windmill could never take to sea, even if it wanted to. It is built of stone and would sink. Indeed, it would collapse if it attempted to move (see *False Vehicle B.S.*). This feeling of unfulfilled hope, that the windmill is struggling to become something it is not, generates *Disappointed Structure B.S.*

Old windmills generate *Change of Use B.S.* when converted into dwellings. The new owners also benefit from *Tower B.S.* and retrospective *Task B.S.*

Piers

Piers are found at the edge of land, like lighthouses, observatories, and windmills. They march into the sea on stilts and so generate *Pole B.S.* You can often see the ocean through gaps in the planks, which provokes *Skeletal B.S.* Piers with restaurants, amusement arcades, or theatres at the end produce *Out on a Limb B.S.* Sadly, many piers are disused and have fallen into disrepair. They can look like the remains of a slim-boned aquatic dinosaur. One pier sold planks to raise money for repairs. The sponsor received an engraved brass plaque fixed to the wood. Their name would be exposed to the elements for years—a B.S. gift if ever there was one.

Oil Rigs

Oil rigs are rather like high-tech, free-standing piers. They are very exposed. Some stand alone, miles out in the North Sea. In size, these marine refuges rival small villages. They are reminiscent of anchored ships, triggering *False Vehicle B.S.*

Water Towers

Water towers are the opposite of oil rigs—they stick up, full of water, in the middle of dry land. It is safer not to think about converting one into a dwelling.

Airports

Airports are firmly rooted in the land, but linked to distant places (see *Station B.S.*). Wandering around them, especially in the early hours of the morning, does terrible things to the bowels. Vast numbers of people pass through airports, most of them suffering from the *Travelling B.S.*

Airport control towers are like huge bay windows that look out onto runways. Besides being close to traffic, like real bay windows, they also control aircraft and so generate *Remote Control B.S.*

Churches

Churches can be very bowel churning. They are often isolated—and frequently surrounded by graves. Their interiors are cool, monumental, and discomforting. There may be crypts beneath them that generate *Secret Passage B.S.* And when there is no one around, churches provoke extreme *Empty Building B.S.* The grand doorways, vaulted ceilings, and large, high windows make a person feel small, like a child again (see *Childhood & The B.S.* and *Childhood Perspective B.S.*).

Pews are normally fixed, and so create a potent version of *Sitting B.S.* Sometimes, pews have radiator pipes running underneath them in a vain attempt to keep the congregation warm. Such under-powered heaters in large spaces create *Inadequate Machine B.S.* I once saw mobile gas heaters in an isolated country church that looked like a procession of aliens marching up the aisle.

Church halls and community rooms can be very B.S., especially those with pronounced echoes and wooden chairs stacked along the walls. The prospect of taking a chair from the stack and sitting in the middle of a deserted church hall is delectable.

Castles

Castles evoke a bowel-twitching suspense. They are refuges with thick stone walls that make them secure against external threats, but they are big enough to contain hidden dangers. The impenetrability of the external walls makes an internal attack hard to escape from. The safe house becomes a trap (see *Refuge-Trap B.S.*). Secret passages and rooms can also be used by enemies, which magnifies the *Refuge-Trap B.S.* Castles are usually uncomfortable: they are functional places full of corridors and huge, difficult-to-heat rooms (see *Childhood Perspective B.S.*). Their gut-tugging architecture is augmented by suits of armour (possibly occupied), draped tapestries, and chests (that may conceal intruders).

Films exploit the castle effect. Huge chambers are dotted with normal-scale furnishings: severe and unpadded seats stand to attention by arched doorways, and comfortable winged armchairs huddle near a monumental fireplace. The action centres on the little oasis of warmth and security near the hearth, which looks like a section of a cosy drawing room transplanted into the castle. This displaced region floats in the vast coolness of the hall. The people near the fire warm their backs against the flames and drink toasts, blithely ignorant of the hazards lurking in the shadows. One by one, the characters troop off to their widely scattered bedrooms. They separate and make themselves easy prey.

Scottish castles near lochs are very B.S., partly because of *Proximity to Water B.S.*, which is amplified in Scottish lochs because of stories of monsters.

Drive-in Cinemas

It is surprising that drive-in cinemas are not more popular, since they are so bowel wracking. Watching a film is usually an indoor experience, so outdoor cinemas trigger *Indoor–Outdoor B.S.*

Deserted drive-ins are dismal zones dotted with small poles (*Pole B.S.*) bearing radio receivers (*Telecommunications B.S.*), and small heaters (*Inadequate Machine B.S.*). Imagine being the only patron at a remote drive-in, watching a horror film while a storm rages.

Pump Stations

Pump stations at dams are isolated, mechanical, and next to an elemental force—water. The vast volumes of fluid passing through pipes under pressure suggest the bowel.

Control Rooms

Controls operating distant equipment generate *Telecommunications B.S.* and *Remote Control B.S.* They may be in cosy, well-lit rooms, filling a corner of a large building or, worse still, in a separate hut. In some cases, the controls may be lost in a forest of other equipment, which provokes *Wired-Up B.S.*

Old science fiction films may show banks of gauges and switches that control distant and powerful machinery—maybe a silvery rocket on a launch pad or a chemical works that threatens to turn critical. Technicians with clipboards trudge along walkways made of metal mesh (generating *Skeletal B.S.*) and lights flash. The B.S. of these images is enhanced if they are in black and white.

Refineries & Chemical Processing Plants

Refineries often form a backdrop to violent action in films. The machinery is heavy-duty, mysterious, and apparently dangerous. Flares go off, and cars frequently career around them. The strange chemical reactions and the periodic or continuous venting of excess gas recall internal processes. The plants seem almost alive.

Factories

Factories are the architectural embodiment of *Task B.S.* Brick factories are best when disused and downtown. These industrial places are steeped in years of toil. All those people trudging in each morning, doing a hard day's work, then wending their way home, make the places magnetic. If only those long-ago workers knew they were contributing to a future B.S. experience—that their drudgery would be elevated to art.

Older factories may have had a central engine that conveyed power to the individual machines via driveshafts and belts.

Imagine a drum factory with a showroom at the top of a tower. A semicircle of windows displays a splendid set of drums. At night, this elevated shop window is a blaze of lights. The drum kit seems to hover like an insectile spacecraft. The B.S. is enhanced by a nearby railway line, industrial buildings, and a public swimming pool. Imagine playing these drums with no one listening except a friend who had sneaked into the closed pool and was listening in on a mobile phone.

Schools

Schools are the training ground for many emotions, and they offer a complex bouquet of B.S. elements. Imagine wandering around a deserted school (preferably one you attended), peeping into empty classrooms, and crossing the echoing assembly hall. Deep-seated emotions soon bubble up.

The quietness makes you feel super late for lessons, giving a thrilling sense of truancy. Being an adult, you can never return to the classroom. You are so incredibly late for school that you have grown up and cannot fit back in. This inability to return to a familiar place—like returning home to find that your house has shrunk—generates *False Refuge B.S.* There is a profound feeling of having missed the boat that verges on the erotic. Revisiting your school emphasises your adulthood and provokes *One Way Vehicle B.S.*

Restaurants

Restaurants, especially fashionable ones, seem designed to provoke the B.S. In some, tables stand next to huge glass windows, obliging patrons to dine in full view. Eating while exposed to the world creates a strong form of *Sitting B.S.* called *Feeding B.S.*

Restaurants that straddle motorways, with traffic passing underneath, generate *Pole B.S.*, *Station B.S.*, and *Proximity to Traffic B.S.*

Coffee Shops

Coffee shops appear in appallingly bowel-gripping situations like bus interchanges, or on the ground floors of office blocks. Those on a corner or next to an entrance are worst of all (see *Proximity to Traffic B.S.*).

Coffee shops inside other buildings (like shopping malls, museums, large department stores, art galleries, zoos, cinemas, and bookshops) generate *Embedded Building B.S.* I have even seen one on the second floor of a furniture warehouse on an industrial estate.

Tables outside create a *B.S. Cascade*. This effect is weak in a square or piazza, but intolerable on a busy road or near a bus shelter.

Hot coffee also stirs the bowels, making cafés even more gut-wrenching. Students, writers and intellectuals often work—or appear to work—in cafés and so add *Task B.S.*

to this potent brew. No wonder so many good ideas come over a cup of coffee.

Follies

Follies include isolated towers, three-sided houses, and other whimsies. These paradoxical and romantic structures can appear in the gardens of stately homes, near roads, in fields, or in public parks. They often look like sections of larger buildings that have uncoupled and drifted away. Some have a slightly fortified appearance.

Imagine a square tower that stands all alone, just above the lakes in a public park. It has a dovecote with entrances for the birds high up. There does not seem to be a normal door, and the place looks as if it has been shut for years.

Pubs

People assemble at a pub to drink and socialise. Like animals at a watering hole, they are nervous. Unsavoury elements may walk in at any time. A pub looks warm and inviting but—being open to the public—has its dangers and so generates *False Refuge B.S.* Some pubs have extreme and overblown decorations, like second-hand books and dusty Victoriana, that are presumably there to emphasise homeliness and to compensate for the public nature of the room.

By contrast, the English country pub or inn can be an exquisitely tasteful refuge. Half-timbered ones that nestle in the countryside can be gorgeously bowel-throbbing. However, a town pub can also be very B.S. The effect is stronger if it stands on a corner and there is a bus stop nearby.

Pubs may display accumulations of pipes, jugs, brasses, cigarette cards, or antiques and so generate *Collection B.S.* Those that look like a junk shop with a bar generate *Feeding B.S.* by introducing food and drink into an unexpected context.

The comfort of the pub is short-lived because eventually one must leave and go home. Like cafés, pubs are the modern equivalent of a watering hole, a place where it is nice to be, but where it is prudent to keep an eye open for predators.

Towers

Towers provide refuge and give a good view of the surrounding countryside. In this respect they resemble lone trees and so evoke a powerful *Primitive B.S.*

Mobile Buildings

Mobile homes are very B.S. They may even have small gardens enclosed by a picket fence. The whole assemblage, less the garden, is movable—a home that follows you, just like in the spaceship fantasy. When connected to the mains, they are locked in place by plumbing, which excites *Anchored B.S.*

Temporary offices and classrooms also create *Task B.S.* Some offices, especially those on construction sites, are on stilts and so generate *Pole B.S.*

Bookshops

Bookshops are very bowel stirring, especially second-hand ones. They can be found in excruciating locations such as arcades, under stairs, nestled in cinemas, or near lifts. Some bookshops have a café attached.

Libraries

Libraries tend to be large public buildings full of books that, apart from anything else, generate *Collection B.S.* Some may provide secluded areas for study in an otherwise public place. Specialist libraries may rent out cubicles for this purpose. Imagine belonging to such a library whilst living in another country and organising to rent a cubicle with no intention of ever visiting it.

Lock-up Garages

Owning a lock-up garage that is distant from your house is very B.S. Owning several is worse. Imagine owning scores of them, forming a necklace of refuges around the world.

As part of a B.S. lifestyle, you could live in a cheap rental property (filled with fine furniture) and keep your very expensive car locked up in a garage several blocks away. You might even have cars hidden away in garages in several cities. You could visit the cities by train and then get a bus or taxi to your garage, preferably at night.

You might even eschew a house altogether, preferring to live in cheap hotel rooms. If you fitted small beds in your garages and plumbed in toilets, then you could happily survive without recourse to a normal dwelling at all. You could equip one with a computer, telephone, and fax machine and run your business from it (a post office box several miles away would act as your address).

Lock-up garages are more B.S. when located in rough suburbs (threat of attack) or in industrial areas (deserted at night and over the weekend).

Buildings that Resemble Vehicles

Buildings that resemble vehicles are B.S. because they suggest a means of escape but fail to deliver (see *False Vehicle B.S.* and *Impeded Vehicle B.S.*). Examples include observatories that look like earthbound spaceships and windmills that strain against the wind like landlocked sailing ships. Some yacht clubs, naval buildings, department stores, and hotels can have curved walls, balconies that wrap around, towers, or even circular windows, which make them uncomfortably reminiscent of the superstructure of ships. Contrariwise, ship superstructures can be discomforting because they look like orphaned buildings that were press-ganged into service.

Moving House

BUILDINGS THAT YOU ONCE LIVED IN but are now deserted are excruciatingly B.S. Usually, new occupants move in quickly, but in the case of our house in Eldershaw Place, the building remained empty for some time. It was a university house in an estate of university houses, and the vacancy rate was quite high (see *Empty City B.S.*). I used to wander past it and contemplate our time there. This was particularly poignant, since the bulk of this book was written there in the small office-cum-bedroom. An excellent fantasy was to imagine reinstalling the computer, either in its original place or perhaps in the middle of the sitting room (see *Wired-Up B.S.*), and continuing to write the book. A case of new draughts in an old house. There would, of course, be none of the familiar home comforts. To amplify this *B.S. Fantasy*, it helped to imagine bringing in a toilet roll attached to a dispenser on wheels. The computer and temporary toilet roll (it would have been more permanent to use the wall-mounted holder) are the very least that are needed to function and so, in addition to the other types of disturbance, there would be *Minimal Camping B.S.*

Revisiting a suburb in which you once lived is a strange experience. When your former house is deserted, but you have no access to it, then you feel like a spirit that has returned to haunt its former residence. It is, in a sense, the obverse of *Haunted House B.S.,* for now you are the haunter, detached and able to impinge in only the faintest way on a world that has moved on.

The Toxic Cottage

Having left Eldershaw, we moved into our own house. The place was dilapidated, but we fell in love with it. Unfortunately, no amount of infatuation could hide the inherent tension between the utilitarian style of construction (concrete and steel) and the cottage-like décor (heavy floral wallpaper and lined curtains). The previous owners left an imposing oak corner cabinet, with a matching bureau-cum-bookcase and a carved wooden three-piece suite. These solid and high-quality pieces jarred with the fabric of the building, in the same way that a fine antique bureau would look out of place in a lock-up garage.

The house was damp and the wallpaper was peeling in places. It had a strong air of decadence, for despite its dereliction, it had clearly been loved in the past. It was like an ersatz English cottage that had been transplanted to the other side of the world (it might have been built in England and then transported to Australia, like many other prefabricated buildings).

We began to slowly renovate our little house. The wallpaper in the main bedroom was stripped and the mould scrubbed from the walls. Gaps between the concrete panels were revealed and had to be filled. The windows were stripped of their white paint, revealing a mixture of beautiful timbers. They were sash windows, except that instead of concealed sashes running inside the window frames, the windows were supported by metal springs coiled inside metal tubes.

Removing the paint, especially the adherent layers on the outside of the frames, was tedious and difficult. A heat gun and an electric drill fitted with a rotary sander were used relentlessly until the gorgeous wood was revealed. The windows were then stained and lacquered. The window furniture was replaced with brass fittings that glowed like gold. Everything else was painted and the floor was stained. The result was spectacular. The main bedroom became glorious and bright, a jewel set in dank concrete.

When we had recovered sufficiently from this exertion, we decided to tackle the lounge room. We began in much the same way, stripping wallpaper and sanding windows. Unfortunately, we discovered lead in the paint and had to abandon the house. We fled, *in medias res,* leaving things just as they were, like a concrete *Mary Ce-leste* (see *Empty Vessel B.S.*).

Henceforth, life took on a surreal and exaggerated B.S. quality. The house was left largely undisturbed and became a forbidden place, generating a potent *Scene of Crime B.S.* The paper peeling from the walls revealed old layers of paint and areas of naked concrete (*Dissection B.S.*). Paint scrapers, screwdrivers, drills and other tools were scattered around, creating *Task B.S.* A vacuum cleaner stood stalwart and abandoned in the middle of the lounge room carpet, like a mechanical soldier overwhelmed by an invisible enemy, its belly full of poison.

What was once a safe and secure home now became a source of fear. An unseen poison pervaded the place. The two armchairs and the settee were displaced towards the middle of the lounge room. They stood jumbled together, quietly toxic yet inviting, beckoning the visitor to sit and make-believe that the room was a safe and comfortable place. It was a macabre scene.

The fear of lead dust transformed the house and made objects that hitherto had been part of everyday life untouchable. One feared to pick up the books, drink from the cups, or cuddle the soft toys. An invisible barrier separated us from everything that was familiar in a severe *Post-Holocaust B.S.* We moved through the house like ghosts (*Haunter B.S.*). The place became a grotesque simulacrum of our home—an obscene museum piece we were forced to traipse through. This sense of detachment was horrendously bowel wracking and augmented by *Empty Building B.S.*, with all that this implied.

Things were made more discomforting by our choice of temporary accommodation, for we moved into Wright Place, only two doors away from our old house in Elder-shaw Place. The house was very similar to Eldershaw, and it felt as if we were living in a reconstruction of the past (*Museum B.S.*) or, worse still, had slipped sideways into a parallel universe. Most things were the same, but certain details were different. This sense that there has been a lateral shift in the environment, a subtle alter-ation in the fine details, is disturbing because it suggests the presence of a predator. The carpets in Eldershaw Place had been changed from the speckled yellow and brown to pale blue, but those in Wright Place were still the old speckled brown variety, making Wright Place more like the old house than the revamped Eldershaw itself. This turned it into an idealised model of the house where the bulk of this book was written. It made me feel like a waxwork of myself, hunched in an attitude of toil, in a museum diorama of my old study. This feeling of history repeating itself was quite disturbing. There was a sense of entrapment, of being caught in a loop, like a rat in a maze.

For several weeks after we fled from our house, the tele-phone line remained connected. The set had an answer-ing machine and fax, enabling it to take messages and print out letters. I could interrogate the machine remote-ly from another phone and listen to the recorded messages, but to make calls or collect faxes I had to undergo special visits to the house. These trips were not easy in the contemplation or the doing.

Visiting our house was like going to an isolated, cavernous, dank, and dishevelled telephone box. The associated directories, address book, and notepad lay on the dining table. Since the exodus, it had been moved next to the telephone table and was now partially blocking the entrance to the kitchen. Together, these surfaces formed a minimal makeshift office that stood clear of the contaminated carpet (*Task B.S.* and *Pole B.S.*). The thought of the phone still operating in an abandoned and toxic house was so bowel tugging and inconvenient that I had the line transferred to Wright Place.

To choose the best course of action, it was necessary to have the house evaluated by a lead expert. My wife and I helped. Carefully, this determined trio poked and prodded and scraped and measured and photographed what was once our home. It was like wandering around a crashed spaceship, trying to find out what had gone wrong (*Investigation B.S.*). The expert used an X-ray machine to probe the lead levels in the paint. This small and sophisticated device displayed interesting spectra, and stored these and the lead levels in its memory. We felt like anthropologists from the future, using advanced technologies to probe an ordinary dwelling.

Checking the fitments of a home in such detail also recalled the childhood interest in the structure of everyday objects. Measuring and recording the lead content of various paint surfaces also smacked of an obsessive need to catalogue and model. Kitchen cabinets and doorframes rarely get this sort of attention. The search for lead was also bowel stirring in that it involved inspecting an apparently safe environment for traces of hazards, a core activity of the B.S. Detecting the underlying layers of lead paint was thrilling in an archaeological sense and disquieting in a toxic one. I suppose that a similar feeling must hit the belly of an Egyptologist who uncovers a wondrous tomb, but fears that a curse may have been unleashed in the process.

I returned to our house on a regular basis to do our laundry, since the washing machine was still there and Wright Place lacked one. It seemed deliciously perverse to do the washing in a contaminated house. Having our lives spread between two houses also meant that our possessions were dispersed, like the aftermath of a wreck.

So perfect and intense was the B.S. generated by the toxic cottage that it made me think it could not be accidental—that this episode was an exquisite nemesis visited on me for having had the temerity to write about bowel stirring things and so conjure demons that should have been left undisturbed. There was a terrible, if impractical, temptation to leave the house as it was and turn it into a monument to the B.S. Its walls hung with black and white close-up photographs of chipped and peeling paint. Badly affected doorframes and window sills

turned into exhibits, framed, glazed, labelled and carefully lit. Small explanatory notices would be positioned
on doors, skirting boards, and window frames. Sections
of carpet might be suspended in glass boxes, with the
contaminated dust extracted and displayed. Soil samples
from front and back could be shown to great advantage
in tightly sealed jars. These could be stood on tiny
shelves, each only sufficient to hold one jar, that were
screwed into unlikely places such as five inches above
the floor in the middle of the hallway, or a foot below the
ceiling in the back bedroom. One of the metal doorframes could be sectioned to demonstrate the red primer
and a cushion from the settee could be opened and
glazed. Tiny brass plaques attached to each exhibit could
be engraved with useful details to help the visitor make
sense of the house, while new and comfortable stools
could be provided for them to sit on while they contemplated their discomforting surroundings. These stools
would not be the conventional free-standing variety but
would be attached to metal arms that projected from the
walls and doorframes. The comfort of the visitor would
be further assured by having a small espresso machine
plumbed into a bar that was built in the entrance hall.

Machine B.S.

MACHINES PERFORM TASKS and extend human capabilities, and so can offer protection or refuge. In their supporting role and in their occasional failure to perform, they can induce the B.S. In usurping the helpful roles of animals—cars replacing horses, for example—machines sometimes trigger the fear that they might rebel against their human operators, like resentful beasts. The section *Machines on the Verge of Becoming Sentient* explains this primitive fear of animation.

Some machines resemble animals quite closely. They have lifespans comparable to domesticated animals. They move around, make noises, consume fuel, emit noxious gases, dribble offensive fluids, need care and attention, and are prone to failure. They can be decked out in fancy livery and decorated to attract attention. They can be sleek and sexy, strong and heavy, humble and workaday, sedentary and methodical, or fast and furious. Machine design also seems to evolve in a biological fashion. With so many animal-like qualities, it is not surprising that the human operator can develop an emotional bond with his machine.

Because so much reliance is placed on machines, separation from them causes great anxiety. In comic strips and in movies, characters may use rockets or other flying devices on their backs. When the hero enters the domain of the arch enemy, the rocket pack may be discarded. There is the overwhelming feeling that it will be gone when he returns. This could be an updated version of a fear of horse thieves.

As well as substituting for animal bodies, machines can become virtual (or real) appendages of human bodies. A pogo stick extends our legs, while night-vision glasses extend our eyes. When we rely on these extensions of the body, we might fear an electrical or mechanical breakdown as we used to fear disease or injury. Dependence on a machine breeds resentment and anxiety, and the fear of it failing generates *Unreliable Machine B.S.*

Imaginary machines often play central roles in B.S. fantasies, acting as plausible mechanisms to allow impossible things. In a fantasy, a visualisable machine is more convincing than pure magic for making things happen and has the advantage that it can act as a B.S. object in its own right. Normal physical rules can be ignored and machines can be dreamt up that are free from the physical constraints and corruptions of the world. Spaceships of unlimited power and storage capacity can transport entire households to distant planets. Flying chairs can carry people above the rooftops, defying wind and gravity. And time machines allow visits to forbidden or inaccessible places. The machines that populate B.S. fantasies can be powered by engines that do not wear out or require refuelling. Cars can be built to extraordinary specifications out of alloys that do not corrode. Boats that cannot sink, built of materials that do not rot, can toss their occupants about on violent oceans in perfect safety. None of these machines could exist in the real world, but B.S. fantasies are full of them. Impossible to construct in a consistent universe, these fabulous inventions can offer a level of security and adventure that real objects cannot match.

Machines on the Verge of Becoming Sentient

Machines that suggest they are on the verge of becoming sentient are B.S., presumably because they evoke a primitive fear of unknown life-forms, or because they seem to threaten their operators in the same way that liberated slaves threaten their masters. The more mechanical in appearance, the better, since their threat seems more physical. High-powered computers (that are presumably more likely to suddenly become conscious) fail in this respect, since they look so elegant and passive (see *Primitive Machines*, below). However, in all highly sophisticated systems, including computers and communication networks, there is a fear of dealing with a potentially hostile intelligence. A machine seems more implacable than an animal, and the chances of escape or appeasement are lower. Because of its very otherness, a machine can give the impression of having an alien and unfathomable intellect.

Decaying Machines that Suggest Disease

A decaying machine might give the impression of being diseased. The bowels recoil from the object to protect us from infection. The bigger the machine, the more powerful the effect. Perhaps this is because we assume the disease was more virulent. Our reaction depends on believing, at some level, that the machine is, or was, alive. This is an example of how the workings of the B.S. are symbolic and why it is necessary to adopt poetic reasoning to understand what is happening.

Decaying Machines that Lose Security

Machines wear out and so emphasise change, failure, and death. We might see in these sad devices a dark foreshadow of our own mortality. If machines supply a valuable service, their failure generates *Inadequate Machine B.S.* If machines offer refuge, their decay triggers *False Refuge B.S.*, while rotting transport devices generate *Impeded Vehicle B.S.* Examples include rusty farm machinery left in the corner of a field, an old car that has rotted in a garage for twenty years, and an aeroplane recovered from a swamp. As with apparently diseased machines, the more massive and powerful the apparatus, the more security is lost when it decays, and the stronger the B.S.

Decaying Machines that Elicit Nostalgia

A decaying or broken machine can be a potent reminder of times past and evoke a strong sense of history. Such a machine has a limited future and so the moments spent with it seem more precious than those spent with a well-preserved piece in a museum or an old but functioning machine that is still operating in its natural environment. This sympathy for discarded and unfortunate devices also occurs in *Disappointed Structure B.S.*

Rusting cars piled up in a scrapyard seem suffused with memories. It is as if these discarded members of the family can still recall their trips to the beach and commutes to the office. The sagging driver's seat retains the imprint of a travelling bottom, while the torn leather in the back could have witnessed nights of passion. The thoughts that passed through the mind of the motorist as he sailed down a country lane, or sat fuming in a traffic jam, echo faintly round the cabin. This warm human emotion, rapidly going cold, gives a forlorn feeling that something has been switched off. A similar feeling of haunting occurs in any wreck.

In Hawaii, there is a fashion for leaving vehicles, or parts of them, to rot by the roadside, where they become covered in luxuriant undergrowth.

Decaying Machines that Threaten to Return to Life

Some decaying machines are reminiscent of corpses and trigger a mild analogue of the ancient horror of the dead returning to life. The similarity to a dead body is stronger when internal components that look vaguely anatomical are exposed. These might include bulkheads, ribs, internal plumbing, electrical wiring, and conduits. Lights and portholes amplify the effect because they look like eyes, while air intakes suggest a mouth. The response is stronger if the location is dramatic and dangerous. A deep-sea trench is ideal, but a river bank or a forest will do. For example, a crashed plane, whose torn fuselage reveals internal struts, can look like a dead dragon, while a shipwreck can look organic if holes in its hull display ribs and bulkheads attached to the keel (see *Dissection B.S.*).

It might seem fanciful to suggest that these hulks provoke a fear of mechanical zombies, but it fits rather well with other bowel stirring reactions. These wrecks have many similarities to dead animals and so can trigger a system which evolved to respond to subtle cues. An alternative explanation is that these corpse-like wrecks can trigger the fear of a visit by an extant relative of a dead predator (the predator's mate could return and devour us). It is as though we unconsciously construct a story to which only our bowels respond. The detective who solves a crime relying on a gut feeling may be using a similar mechanism.

Damaged Machines Suggesting a Predator

Damaged machines provoke the fear that they are victims of a predator that still lurks in the vicinity. Approaching such a machine generates a bowel-wrenching fear that something will jump out and attack. This feeling occurs strongly when wrecks are investigated. Swimming around a sunken ship might raise fears of sharks or giant squid. Approaching an Earth rocket that has crash-landed on another planet could elicit a fear of an attack by aliens.

Abandoned Machines Suggesting a Predator

Abandoned machines could tumble the bowels because they provoke the fear that predators took the operators. It is the machine or vehicle equivalent of *Empty Building B.S.* The ultimate example is *Mary Celeste.*

Damaged Machines that Look like Angry Victims

Some damaged machines look like fallen animals that could lash out if approached. The B.S. warns us to be careful when approaching them. Our ancestors might have felt the same twinge as they advanced on their kill to check that it was dead. A scrapyard full of cars—whose headlights and grilles mimic the eyes and jaws of aggressive beasts—might stir the bowels for this reason.

Sleeping Predator Machines

Some machines, especially quiescent robots, suggest a sleeping predator. Others give the impression of being containers for predators. Wandering around the corridors of an alien spaceship would be discomforting because concealed occupants might leap out. Household appliances, such as fridges and water heaters, that operate thermostatically and so switch themselves on and off in the middle of the night, can also be discomforting for this reason.

Supervention by Machines

Machines that continue to function without human supervision can give the impression that the age of humans has gone, and that the torch of evolution has passed to machines. Consequently, robots can be quite unnerving. There is something faintly sinister about traffic lights that continue to change on an empty road, automatic production lines that operate in deserted factories, and chemical works and oil refineries that grind away and emit smoke and flames without apparent supervision.

Lumbering unmanned vehicles that heave themselves over the landscape like behemoths can look like replacement life-forms and so generate this type of B.S.

Machines of Inadequate Power or Reliability

Inadequate machines can leave you in the lurch if you rely on them for comfort or protection. The B.S. warns you off these dubious devices. Examples include heating devices that are patently too weak for the job in hand (such as a single-element electric fire out of doors), and torches that only offer a weak yellow light to explore a dark crypt. Inferior weapons or armour that expose you to attack have a similar effect.

Unreliable machines can break down just when you need them. Examples include torches that fail, and weapons that run out of ammunition or whose power supply fails. Machines that fail like this sometimes figure in ghost stories. Belonging to the everyday, such machines emphasise the entry into another realm when they give way. Even high-tech equipment can be out of its depth in the presence of supernatural forces.

Inadequately powered or unreliable vehicles are B.S. because they suggest the possibility of escape but cannot deliver. Examples include a flying machine that can only hover when you need it to soar (like a crippled spacecraft trying to leave a hostile planet) or a car that can only limp away from a crowd of zombies (see also *False Vehicle B.S.* and *Impeded Vehicle B.S.*).

Machines that Display their Working Parts

Household appliances and vehicles normally have their working parts hidden away and so we tend to forget about their internal mechanisms. It can be very disturbing when these parts are exposed. Perhaps this echoes the horror of seeing the innards of a living thing exposed by accident, attack, surgery, or investigation (see *Dissection B.S.*).

There was a fashion for transparent household devices that included see-through radios and telephones. These, and other machines whose workings are on display, might resemble museum exhibits and so generate *Framing B.S.* This would be especially true of a device with a window cut into it, or whose opaque casing was replaced by a transparent one.

Dismantled household appliances on a workbench or in a scrapyard have the same quality and tend also to trigger *Wired-Up B.S.*

Vehicles with exposed engines (or other systems) look vulnerable to attack. The B.S. might warn you not to rely on such a vehicle for escape, since something might latch onto the engine and disable it when you are in full flight (see *Impeded Vehicle B.S.* and *External Mechanism B.S.*). Motorbikes can elicit this reaction because their engines hang exposed just above the ground.

Manufacturers rarely attempt to disguise the workings of industrial machines. Lathes, pumps and turbines look like what they are. These "mechanical machines" might be discomforting because they look primitive compared to sleekly packaged domestic appliances (see *Primitive Machines & Evolutionary Convergence*, below). The industrial machine suggests an unproven prototype that is experimental and prone to failure, and generates *Unreliable Machine B.S.* In addition, industrial machines provoke *Task B.S.*

Primitive Machines and Evolutionary Convergence

Early versions of machines tend to exhibit their workings more openly than later varieties, and they may be decorated in bizarre ways. Various designs are tried, some quite aberrant, until a more finished version is settled on. This echoes biological evolution, where a burst of initial variety is gradually whittled down to a few rather uniform species. As their bodies and behaviours are perfected, they tend to converge toward a common type. For example, ancient fish had very bizarre appearances, with bits protruding here and there and occasional armour plating. These appendages have largely gone as selective forces polished the bodies to smoother and sleeker designs. While nature may have sandpapered the fish, an urge for economy has done the same to motor cars through the wind tunnel and the computer model. Now, one or two basic types have replaced the earlier pageant of bizarre models. You must stare and squint to see who made it and how powerful it is.

This homogenisation can be quite frustrating for the motorist who likes to express his personality through the appearance of his vehicle. People still try to personalise their cars with spoilers, mud flaps, headlamp guards, weather shields, sun visors, and Venetian-style louvres. These accessories are flap-like and hark back to the glorious fins lost earlier in automobile evolution.

Perhaps there is only one optimal design of machine for a particular purpose. If so, then how can we differentiate products in the marketplace? Designers, schooled in the B.S., will be called in to personalise and beautify the products of the future. Alternative designs could flourish simply because they are more interesting to look at or use. They would probably be far more expensive to fabricate, less efficient, less reliable, and less elegant, but they would at least add diversity to life. Some products already show these characteristics, notably cheaper stereo equipment (see *Designer B.S.*).

Almost invariably, older and more primitive versions of machines are more B.S. than later models (this applies to buildings and other artefacts too). This *Primitive Machine B.S.* is partly because of the greater number of details and the more obvious working parts, but also reflects the belief that older machines are weaker (see *Machines of Inadequate Power or Reliability* above).

Highly Specialised Machines
Machines that look odd because they are highly specialised can be troubling to contemplate. They tend to be uncompromisingly utilitarian (*Task B.S.*) and may have strange arms, dials, and other appendages that trigger *Primitive Machine B.S.* and *External Mechanism B.S.* Such

devices seem horribly out of place anywhere but their natural environment. Thus a lathe—which properly belongs in a workshop—looks uncomfortable if left in the street.

Highly specialised machines displaced from their work areas seem orphaned. One fears they cannot cope in a varied and hostile environment, rather as an exotic specimen escaping from a menagerie might perish.

The Remote Control of Machines

Remotely controlled machines range from a small model aeroplane flown in a local park to a planetary probe that hauls itself over the surface of a distant world (see *Probe B.S.*). Such devices can work in hostile or inaccessible places without risking the safety of their human operator. However, the person at the controls is likely to imagine being in the machine, and this venture into hostile territory by proxy triggers severe bowel throbbing. As virtual-reality tools become more sophisticated, the sense of being there will increase, and *Remote Control B.S.* will intensify.

Remote-controlled models are exquisitely B.S. Think of a submarine that could sail under the local lake, or a helicopter that could hover around the neighbourhood. Attaching cameras to these models makes them even more B.S. Models fitted with an old mechanical camera could return with a film or plate that needs developing. Those fitted with a video camera could transmit live pictures or return with a tape. Imagine receiving pictures from the bottom of the park lake, or using a helicopter to trace the route you take to work. Even worse, imagine controlling the model helicopter from a foreign country and sending it over the playground of your old junior school. Imagine controlling a small model tank and sending it around a deserted factory to take pictures.

Remote-controlled machines equipped with detection devices are rather like independent sense organs that can be sent off on their own—mechanical deputies that stride fearlessly into the line of fire. Robots that climb into a volcano, prod a bomb, trundle down a pipe, or sit in the hard vacuum of space and never complain. They might occasionally explode or get stuck or miss their trajectory and go careering off into infinity (there is little to match the B.S. of a lost space probe). But they keep their operators safe and they are lovely for the B.S. connoisseur to contemplate.

Logging on to distant computers generates *Remote Control B.S.* and this might help to explain the attraction of international computer networks (see *Telecommunications B.S.*, *Network B.S.* and *Computer Networks, Remote Access and Hacking*).

Emissary Machines

Machines that go off on their own to perform a task or deliver a message elicit *Emissary Machine B.S.*, which is similar to *Remote Control B.S.* but has a slightly different flavour and may have a separate origin. A good example is a space capsule that contains examples of human works (music, art, mathematics, images of earthly life-forms, etc.) and is dispatched in the hope that aliens will discover it and decipher its messages.

A less ambitious project is to stash contemporary items in a canister which is then locked up, buried, or encased in concrete. These "time capsules" are designed for future generations to enjoy—a ready-made archaeology.

This peculiar brand of B.S. would be stronger if the machines constructed objects from local materials when they reached their destinations. They could put on a bit of a show—an extravaganza for an unknown audience on a locally built stage. The space capsule might use alien rocks to build a facsimile of an Earth house, or arrange the rocks to spell Earth words before taking off for the next planet. The time capsule might use contemporary materials to reconstruct life in the twentieth century. In the extreme case, the machines would construct copies of themselves as well. They are like an actor who divides and divides to form a troupe, builds a stage, and puts on a play. One actor then flies off to the next venue to repeat the process.

The parallel with reproductive cells is compelling. Sex cells migrate and then construct new bodies using local materials (food). The machines land and their effects are magnified by the use of local materials. Emissary machines are the egg and sperm of the mind (see *Dissemination of Ideas B.S.*).

Reproduction fits into the predatory theory of the B.S. because avoiding predators helps survival, which in turn allows reproduction. Moreover, sex may have evolved as a strategy to evade predators. This most extreme and attenuated form of B.S. harks back to the very reason for avoiding predators in the first place: to replicate.

Self-Fulfilling Machines

Some contrivances create a need and then satisfy it. Two examples come to mind.

A free-standing toilet roll holder on a pole. This device is so B.S. that it immediately creates an urge to defaecate, and thus makes itself indispensable (an indispensable dispenser).

The other device is a tall tower with a light on top. The function of the tower is to support the light, which in turn prevents aircraft from colliding with the tower.

These machines would never have come into existence save for some perversity of their creator. All machines create their own markets to some extent, but *Self-Fulfilling Machines* are extremely self-contained and insulated from normal market forces (as some art aims to be). These strange objects are sequestered from everyday concerns and have, in a sense, drawn their tentacles in.

Huddled up in their own circular logic, they stir the bowels like an urchin.

Vehicular B.S.

VEHICLES CAN BE A MEANS OF ESCAPE—a role of great importance in the B.S.—and they can also act as moving or stationary refuges. As machines, they trigger various forms of *Machine B.S.* Vehicles whose mechanisms are wearing out can elicit *Unreliable Machine B.S.,* while older vehicles, especially those whose designs were experimental, can evoke *Primitive Machine B.S.*

Vehicles become extremely bowel stirring when they are dramatically out of context, especially when this restricts their movement (see *Impeded Vehicle B.S.*). A ship in dry dock has this effect. Vehicles that are kept indoors can seem trapped, and so they too provoke a version of *Impeded Vehicle B.S.* called *Indoor Vehicle B.S.* This is why vehicles that are being repaired or stored in garages stir the bowels. Examples include an aeroplane in a hangar, locomotives in a shed, and buses in a garage. Transport museums are the extreme version, but many of their exhibits are totally disabled, and so generate the more extreme *False Vehicle B.S.* To complicate matters still further, a vehicle that is inside a building is also a refuge within a refuge and so generates a machine version of *Embedded Building B.S.*

Permanently disabled vehicles, or things that pretend to be vehicular, generate *False Vehicle B.S.* This probably functions as a warning system to stop people from making the mistake of climbing into a vehicle that cannot run. A section of a car projecting above the entrance of a shop would have this effect.

Vehicles on poles are restricted and so generate *Impeded Vehicle B.S.* as well as *Pole B.S.* A small car on a pole in someone's front garden would be hard to pass. Suspended vehicles, or those on stands, are bowel stirring for similar reasons. Workaday vehicles that are prominently displayed can generate *Framing B.S.*

Boats are B.S. because of an ancient fear of attack from below (think how bowel stirring a glass-bottomed boat is). They also make good escape vehicles because they are difficult to follow and are often large enough to carry provisions for a long journey or siege. Boats that look liable to sink are excruciatingly B.S. because our bowels are counselling us against boarding them. This might partly explain our gut-wrenching fascination with shipwrecks.

Flying machines tend to stir the bowels, although I find that modern airliners have little effect. Vintage aeroplanes may provoke *Skeletal B.S.* or *Icarian B.S.*, whereas spaceships can be the ultimate form of refuge from a hostile planet (see *Ark B.S.*). Helicopters can quickly escape from a dangerous situation, and can stir the bowels in anticipation of a getaway. Hovercraft travel just clear of the ground, but have nothing to keep them up when the power is switched off.

Public vehicles, such as buses and trains, tend to be more excruciating than private vehicles like cars. Perhaps this is because their doors are not locked. Indeed, their doors frequently open automatically to admit new passengers, some of whom may be threatening. In this respect, they are like public buildings and lifts. Such vehicles are more B.S. if there has been a change of use or if they are empty (see *Change of Use B.S.* and *Empty Building B.S.*).

Industrial vehicles like lorries, diggers, mobile cranes, road sweepers, and rubbish collectors are quite bowel tumbling as well. They are specialised and utilitarian and their cumbersome and aberrant designs are evocative of the early and unlikely species that lived millions of years ago (see *Primitive Machine B.S.*).

Private cars, being more mass-produced, tend to be less bizarre, but may evoke *Abstract Particular B.S.* Cars are comparable to the sleeker and more general-purpose body types that evolved later. Cars are more successful and populous than their lumbering cousins, but they are less interesting (which is, perhaps, why so many people feel the compulsion to customise them).

Travelling through the night makes any vehicle more B.S., since dangers might lurk in the dark. Riding along a dark suburban street on a push bike with flickering lights is more B.S. than riding the same machine on a sunny afternoon. A boat on a stormy midnight sea is more B.S. than it would be on a calm morning. Even a car returning from a night out (especially if you are a child on the back seat) is B.S.

All vehicles suggest a journey and so provoke some *Travelling B.S.* Loading vehicles with provisions intensifies this feeling. Perhaps this is why children enjoy stashing things into their toy cars or saddlebags. Packing the car for a holiday can bring vague twinges of *Travelling B.S.* into sharp relief. Filling a ship ready for a long voyage, heaving sacks onto a galleon, winching crates onto an Antarctic vessel, or inserting pods into a starship, strongly emphasise the start of a journey. The extreme version of packing for a journey is preparing a vessel for evacuation (see *Ark B.S.*).

Cycles

Pushbikes are B.S. because they extend the speed and range of the human frame without offering much protection. The rider is exposed to all sorts of hazards. There is the fear of being attacked by yobs or big dogs. On a cycle, evading danger depends on muscle power alone. This gives cycles a special brand of B.S. associated with mechanisms that amplify human abilities without adding power themselves. Concern about the chain coming off or getting a puncture adds a touch of *Unreliable Machine B.S.* Cycles are basically moving frameworks (see *Skeletal B.S.*) with their mechanisms exposed to view (see *External Mechanism B.S.*).

A cyclist is acutely aware of the environment in a sensory way. More details are visible from a cycle than from a car, and this intimacy with the landscape can tug at the bowel. After all, the B.S. may have originated in a need to fully appreciate the landscape with its escape routes and other denizens and is associated with a heightened sensibility.

Motorbikes are intermediate between pushbikes and cars and some old types look like pushbikes that have been distorted to accommodate an engine (*Motorised B.S.*). Their pushbike parentage is more obvious when the saddles have visible springs, or when pedals are retained. A motorcyclist must sit in an exposed position, which generates a moving version of *Sitting B.S.* Old motorbikes are more B.S. than later ones because there is little attempt to conceal their workings beneath flashy exteriors. Some motorbikes look quite predatory and have bizarre decorations and so generate *Primitive Machine B.S.* The contrast between the polished machine and the rough ground is very obvious. Shiny parts and complicated devices hang a few inches above the tarmac and so provoke *External Mechanism B.S.* Riding through derelict industrial areas heightens this contrast and increases the B.S.

See *Machines that Display their Working Parts* and *Dissection B.S.*

Scooters tend to hide their workings, but their apparent lack of power, and the ease of mounting and dismounting them, make them closer to the environment through which they travel and therefore more B.S. Scooters on which you must stand, since they lack a seat, are exquisite and only one stage above a motorised pogo stick.

Motorbikes may fail to start. This happens in films when the fugitive desperately tries to kick start the bike as his pursuers close in. Usually, the bike starts just before they get him. I can think of two instances when motorbikes were used as time machines on television programmes, which must mean something.

Cars

Very old cars gain significant B.S. by looking like motorised carriages (see *Motorised B.S.*). Modern cars, by comparison, provoke very little B.S., for they are too slick, and their mechanics too integrated. There is an interesting parallel with computers. Very primitive ones, which fill a room with valves and wires, are very B.S. (see *Primitive Machine B.S.* and *Wired-Up B.S.*), but powerful modern varieties produce little agitation (unless they are located in exceedingly low-tech or temporary buildings). The addition of a car phone can rectify the low level of B.S. of a modern car. It is safer not to contemplate adding a phone to a vintage car!

In older cars, details tend to sprout in ways that no longer apply. Huge lights or wing mirrors project well beyond the general outline. Overall designs are more flamboyant and fantastical, being less constrained by the needs of safety and economy than modern cars. Some cars from the 50s look like earth-bound spaceships, with their rear lights mounted like rocket engines. The image is confused if the car is a convertible (although a spaceship with a pull-down roof would be immeasurably B.S.). Very primitive models from the turn of the century may have wickerwork picnic baskets attached to their mudguards or running boards. It is generally not a good idea to have your food supply housed in an external and insecure container. It is rather like keeping your fridge in the street.

Older cars may need parts that are no longer manufactured. Specialist markets, traders, or scrap yards might be needed. Parts obtained in this way add a nice touch of diversity to the car. Components that emerged from the same factory years ago, but subsequently led very different lives, may be bolted together. Contemplating all the sources and the varied histories of the parts may trigger a B.S. frisson. Rescuing forlorn pieces of machinery (the parts as well as the car itself) from oblivion generates *Liberation B.S.*

Old petrol pumps that stand like lonely figures are excruciatingly B.S. Hollow plastic signs that once lit up with the trade name of the petrol company form the head. The nozzle inserts high at the shoulder as if the pump were clasping its lapel. They may be seen, standing disused and forlorn, on the forecourts of closed garages, like dead robots. Since they so closely resemble human figures, partially dismantled pumps generate a potent form of *Dissection B.S.* Disused petrol pumps might agitate the bowel because they can no longer supply fuel. It would be important to recognise these useless pumps, since they could delay an escape (see *Impeded Vehicle B.S.*). If you were trying to drive away from a crowd of zombies in an open-top sports car, you would not want to stop at such an old pump.

People may collect petrol pumps rather like they collect red telephone boxes.

Buses

Classic double-decker buses are wonderfully B.S. The driver sits isolated in a little cabin with its own entrance. The conductor is separated from the driver and can walk about the bus or stand on the platform at the back. The spiral staircase generates an extraordinary moving version of *Staircase B.S.*, while the permanently open rear is like a porch without a door, giving a delicious sense of exposure to those at the back. These features make a double-decker bus like a mobile house with an open door. Passengers enter and leave like guests at a roving party.

Modern buses are usually single-deckers. They rarely have a conductor, and the driver sits within the body of the bus. They are far less B.S. than the old variety.

Buses have additional B.S. qualities deriving from their routes, timetables, bus stops, ticket offices, and terminals. The bus, its scheduling, paperwork, and the associated structures, form an extended pattern comparable to the mix of routes and refuges in *The Landscape of Potential Toilets*.

It is possible to collect and classify bus tickets, timetables, numbers, and other variable items (see *Collection B.S.*).

Trams

Trams are like buses trying to evolve into trains. Their rails run in the middle of normal roads, which can be highly unsettling to the sensitive bowel. Tram routes are clearly defined by rails and overhead wires, making them far more obvious and concrete than the paths of buses (see *Rail B.S.*).

Trains

A train is like a mobile terrace of houses. A string of refuges pulled along. Trains crossing wide open spaces seem highly vulnerable, like huge lumbering beasts that cannot change direction, even when attacked. The similarity to big game is more pronounced when the trains are pulled by steam locomotives that huff and puff and shriek. The B.S. might warn us not to climb aboard and tie our fate to such limited brutes.

Stations, platforms, signal boxes, signals, and overhead electrical cables are all B.S. Signal boxes are exquisitely bowel wracking. They may stand near a level crossing or beyond the platform and so generate *Proximity to Traffic B.S.* These small refuges are used to control trains and so provoke *Remote Control B.S.*

Locomotives grouped together in sheds, especially if there is a turntable, trigger a violent form of *Indoor Vehicle B.S.* They look like a herd of grazing monsters huddled together for shelter.

Science fiction illustrations from the 1950s often included elevated chute and rail networks in their cities of the future. However, knowing that these transport systems existed only in the imagination generates *False Vehicle B.S.*

Underground Trains

Underground trains are B.S. for many reasons. Confined to tunnels and hidden from the light of day, they provoke *Disappointed Structure B.S.*, while their subterranean existence triggers *Going Underground B.S.* Huge escalators (*Staircase B.S.*) or clanking lifts convey passengers to the underground stations, where they may be assailed by the sight of chocolate vending machines attached to the curved walls. The tunnels themselves may be draped with heavy-duty cables, causing *Wired-Up B.S.*

Traction Engines

Traction engines are huge and lumbering machines that look extremely primitive. Few things can stand in their way, and it is very B.S. to imagine riding one across ploughed fields, through hedges, and across roads. Massive like trains, but free from rails, they make excellent warhorses, like tame mechanical dinosaurs. The fear that they might run amok generates the B.S.

The use of such unlikely and monumental machines for transport might imply a post-holocaust scenario in which weaker vehicles were destroyed. One feels that the people have been forced to break into museums to find machines that are sufficiently robust to operate in the new situation (see also *Liberation B.S.*).

Ships

Boats and ships provide floating refuges that isolate us from terrestrial dangers. However, there is only the hull to separate us from the water—and water contains terrifying predators. Indeed, we seem to have a very basic fear of attack from under the water (see *Proximity to Water B.S.*). Great liners are like floating cities. They form a safe haven in the middle of the ocean and are clearly a form of refuge.

Galleons are supremely B.S. vessels (indeed, all wooden vehicles are B.S.). Perhaps the timbers, masts, yardarms, rigging and sails correspond to features of trees. These elderly boats are like small woods placed in the sea. Climbing the rigging and keeping watch from the crow's nest must be very similar to climbing a tree in the primordial forest and looking out for trouble.

Barges

Barges that travel along canals generate an aquatic version of *Rail B.S.* Those used as homes are extremely bowel-throbbing refuges. The idea of a living room only inches above cold, oily, turbid water is highly discomforting. Having said that, industrial barges are appalling too. A rusting hulk full of coal and veiled by mist on a winter's night is not an easy thing to contemplate, especially if it is moored near a bridge and the nearest dwelling is a boathouse just downriver.

Canals are usually full of stagnant and murky water. They seem strangely unnatural, like impeded rivers. Perhaps waterways are distressing because they make the landscape look tampered with. These watery streets may agitate us because they look like an elaborate trap, or a road system forged by hulking creatures that need water to support their bodies as they cross the land. The locks, and other heavy-duty and specialised machinery, are disturbing too. Canals, being wet things used for transport, may suggest the alimentary tract or a disproportionately large sewage system. A house built next to a canal can make the waterway look like an oversized drain.

It is interesting how canals figure in crime. They seem to attract murderers and rapists (see *Crime B.S.*).

Cable Cars

Cable cars hang above hazardous terrain. Held aloft, they are out of reach of predators but highly visible, creating elements of *Skeletal B.S.* and *Rail B.S.*

Hot Air Balloons

Hot air balloons float quietly above the world, using warm air rather than an engine to keep them aloft. Our bowels are stirred by fear of a forced landing (see *Parachute B.S.*). When a balloon skims over the treetops we worry about what lurks beneath the foliage.

Fire has long been used to scare away predators. In a hot air balloon it also provides the motive force for escape. Unfortunately, fires can go out. This ancient worry about the flame being extinguished provokes *Unreliable Machine B.S.* The flames might just flicker at a low level, and only keep the balloon a few feet above the ground, triggering *Inadequate Machine B.S.* and *Impeded Vehicle B.S.* Travelling in a wickerwork basket with a fire roaring overhead can be compared with sitting in a wickerwork chair in front of a hearth. To get a taste of the sort of B.S. involved, imagine taking the relevant section of your sitting room (fireplace, chimney, part of the floor, and a chair) for a flight above the treetops. You would be an armchair traveller in the fiercest sense.

Hot air balloons derive some B.S. from the fact that they are vehicles made from rather basic materials, such as wickerwork (B.S. in its own right), ropes, and cloth. Nowadays, the materials may be more sophisticated but they are still reminiscent of household goods, the sort of things that you could find in the kitchen (see *Motorised B.S.*).

Home-made flying machines generate a special B.S. Stories sometimes describe these ambitious and secret vehicles. A rocket assembled in the garden shed, or a one-person hovercraft glued and screwed together in the cellar. There is an element of bowel-tingling hubris about constructing such daring and flimsy machines (see *Icarian B.S.*), which might hark back to childhood, when we made things from egg boxes, detergent bottles, and the tubes from toilet rolls.

Telecommunications B.S.

TELECOMMUNICATIONS EQUIPMENT, associated buildings, and related impedimenta are B.S. Many people get tumbling bowels when talking on the telephone and have to cut short their call. When communicating over a long distance—long compared with speaking in person—the apparent distance contracts, bringing the two parties together. We create a living room of the mind to hold the conversation, since we cannot comprehend the vast distances involved (although we still know, at an intellectual level, that a great gulf is being spanned). In this virtual conversation space, two distant places come together, creating an extremely steep *B.S. Gradient*.

Telecommunications equipment might be used to summon help. Indeed, this high-tech cry to the rest of the herd might point to the source of *Telecommunications B.S.* The mayday calls of ships are the classical form, especially when rendered in Morse code as SOS. A more up-to-date example would be calling the police from a car phone while yobs attempted to break in. The call to the rest of the herd might also be altruistic, to warn them of danger.

Telecommunications equipment can also carry general rallying cries—the herd calling all its members, including the outlying ones. This is broadcasting as a force for cohesion. Telecommunications equipment can transmit propaganda and so unify one group against another, especially in times of conflict. Such networking of a group can happen at many levels. Within a family, it can take the form of a car phone that offers additional security for a daughter travelling at night. A professional group might link up using electronic mail or gather for an interactive satellite broadcast. A nation might watch the same television news. Ultimately, our entire species is enmeshed in a telecommunications web. Using or contemplating this network emphasises our commonality. We all belong to the same species, as distinct from predators that belong to other species (see *Network B.S.*).

The pathways taken by the data, when imagined, are like potential routes of escape. In a sense, a message is escaping (see *Emissary Machines*). The world is now criss-crossed by these data lines that offer a degree of comfort. However, when we call someone else, it may remind us of our isolation and thereby agitate us.

Telecommunications Satellites

Telecommunications satellites are very B.S. They sit out in space and relay conversations or other data. It must be a very lonely existence. Imagine being up there in the satellite, far from everyone else but connected to Earth by thousands of unseen telephone links.

Receiving a message relayed by satellite is B.S. when you imagine the journey the words took into space. International phone conversations can thus stir the bowels, as the route taken by the words—from sitting room to satellite to sitting room—is imagined. It would be even more discomforting to talk from a public telephone box, knowing that your words go, via satellite, to someone's sitting room.

Undersea Cables

Undersea cables lie on a very alien and forbidding surface. It is B.S. to imagine that every word in a conversation travels along the deep valleys, wide plains and high mountains of the ocean bed, and that weird aquatic life forms swim, glide, and throb over the cable as we speak. High above, storms rage over the waves, and boats, lit up and full of passengers, cruise by.

The laying of undersea cables by the old steamships must have been a very B.S. enterprise (see *Pioneering B.S.*). The cable created a direct connection to the land, along the ocean floor, which triggers an extended version of *Anchored B.S.*

Land stations that send cables out to sea are very B.S. (see *Station B.S.*).

Telephones

Telephones are exceedingly B.S. The older varieties are worse because they are more mechanical, especially Bakelite ones with twisted, fabric-covered wires. The location of a telephone greatly influences its level of B.S. One in an external telephone box on a windy street corner is fantastically B.S., whereas a modern digital handset in a comfortable lounge room causes much less turbulence. The first obvious B.S. experience of many people involves cutting short a telephone call because of a more urgent call of nature. Shyness, embarrassment and anxiety may also play a part in telephone use. Courtship and other forms of persuasion frequently require the telephone. Pity the poor adolescent trying to arrange a first date using a public phone.

Telephone Boxes

Telephone boxes not only contain telephones, but they are refuges in the street. Directories increase the B.S. because they give the box a slightly homely feel, in the same way that a shelf of books makes a room more cosy. Unfortunately, this only emphasises that the telephone box is not a real room, which increases the sense of exposure. Some telephone boxes are not fully enclosed, and are therefore excruciatingly B.S. They have no clear boundary, and so the caller does not know whether he is inside or outside, and he finds himself poised on a B.S. cusp. Examples of this type of shelter can be seen clustering in certain pedestrian precincts.

Telephone boxes inside buildings (see *Embedded Building B.S.*) may be little more than partial hoods that offer limited sound insulation. They occur near lifts or under stairwells in hotels, airports, stations and the like. The degree of enclosure of the box is subject to fashion like the length of skirts. Originally, the trusty red telephone box was like a little house—solid and concealing, like the long, heavy skirts of many years ago. Modern "boxes" may be little more than handsets on poles (perhaps with a small roof attached), the telephonic equivalents of string bikinis.

Telephone boxes provoke criminal responses: people urinate in them, write all over them, smash them up, and steal the directories. Perhaps the limited mind, when confronted by a B.S. structure, simply lashes out (see *Crime B.S.*). Civilised people—who are more likely to appreciate and cope with the B.S.—may even collect telephone boxes (in which, I suppose, they are at liberty to do whatever they like).

Telephone directories, being links to many addresses, are B.S. things. In helping us to navigate in a telephonic world, they generate *Map B.S.* In gathering together so many names, they trigger *Collection B.S.* It is interesting that conceptual artists may use directories as sources of inspiration.

Fax Machines & Faxes

Like all machines connected to the telephone network, fax machines are B.S. The effect is strengthened if the device sits in a deserted place. Imagine one on a service counter in a department store on the top floor, between the soft furnishings, kitchen appliances and electronic goods. Then imagine it receiving an overseas transmission late at night, when everyone has gone home.

Faxes are B.S. because they are images that have travelled over vast distances, perhaps along undersea cables or out in space via telecommunications satellites. Contemplating a route through such hostile regions generates the B.S. At an intellectual level, we understand that only a data stream has travelled, but the B.S.—operating at a more primitive and visceral level—suggests that the paper itself has been transported, like instant letter post.

Broadcasting & Receiving Equipment

Radio and television transmission towers perched on hills are very B.S. They are isolated and exposed to the sky (*Lightning Conductor B.S.*) yet they are in touch with many distant receivers. Dramatic, skeletal, and slightly robotic, they are reminiscent of sentinels watching the city.

Old radio sets—the wooden ones full of valves and bits of wire—are wonderfully B.S. Imagine trying to locate a faraway station late on a winter's night. The valves glow and the dial emits a pale yellow light. A storm roils outside and dinner is cooking downstairs. As well as *Telecommunications B.S.*, there is an element of *Primitive Machine B.S.* in these archaic receivers.

Old black and white television sets are B.S. because a flickering image, especially one with atmospheric interference, looks as if it had difficulty crossing the ether. The degraded picture emphasises the distance that it has travelled (by contrast, a high-fidelity colour image is clean and pure). The viewer may even have the impression that the television set is a window onto somewhere very distant. Looking at the set is like peering through a telescope. This may explain part of the nostalgic appeal of old black and white films—they give the impression we are seeing real past events through a time telescope, the colour having been filtered out by the thickness of the years.

When viewing an old black and white television, we may feel it is receiving pictures transmitted from when the set was first built. The same would hold true for an old radio. The receiver seems lodged in that period, like a time machine or conduit to a secure past.

Things that have considerable personal significance can provoke the B.S. when they are viewed on a television set many miles away. An example of this is catching glimpses of home when you live on the other side of the world. In Australia, I watched a cricket or football match broadcast from Northampton in England. I saw the roofs of some houses in Abington Avenue, the street where I grew up, and I was greatly moved (I have no interest in football or cricket and I only watched the program for nostalgic and B.S. reasons). The B.S. effect is much more pronounced if the broadcast is live, since then there is the feeling of real contact. The contrast between England and Australia is very strong, for the seasons, as well as night and day, are inverted. On a warm summer's night, you could watch a live match played on a winter's afternoon in your home town.

An interesting B.S. exercise is to rent a video and play it when the same film is being broadcast. This perverse behaviour (apart from excluding adverts) generates a strange form of *In Transit in Parallel B.S.*, because the signals being read from your tape, and the signals being broadcast, originated in the same place, but they arrive by different routes.

Computer Networks, Remote Access and Hacking

From the comfort of your own room, you can probe a distant computer, which is very B.S. In a sense, you visit the other machine (see *Probe B.S.*). This is rather like teleportation, or projecting yourself into a distant office. Being part of an electronic community generates *Network B.S.* The ability to interact with the distant computer increases the illusion of being there and provokes *Remote Control B.S.*

Hacking, being an illicit rummage through someone else's material, is a form of virtual trespass. It is highly disturbing because it combines *Trespass B.S.* with *Remote Control B.S.*, *Network B.S.*, and *Telecommunications B.S.*

Wired-Up B.S.

Untidily placed electrical or electronic equipment can generate *Wired-Up B.S.* This can happen whilst equipment is being installed. Wires go everywhere, panels are opened up, holes are drilled, tools lie around, and the place is a bit of a mess (see also *Dissection B.S.*). When everything is cleared away and the equipment is neatly installed, *Wired-Up B.S.* declines. The re-wiring of a house or the fitting of a telephone network in an office are good examples. Watching major works, such as the installation of a television studio, is even more unsettling for the sensitive bowel.

Wired-Up B.S. also occurs when apparatus is set up temporarily. Equipment installed for a particular job will do this. A filming session can render a place B.S. by strewing equipment around. Loudspeaker systems set up for rallies or rock concerts have the same effect. Knowing that everything will soon be loaded into cases and taken away also generates *Temporary Structure B.S.*

Workshops can be full of *Wired-Up B.S.* Equipment may be littered about, with wires draped everywhere. Things that are in for repair may be partially dismantled and have probes sticking out of them. Such places can look like hospitals for machines. Laboratories can generate *Wired-Up B.S.* when apparatus is set up to conduct an experiment. As the work progresses, the apparatus might be re-wired or re-configured, and so always appears untidy, at least to an outsider. Mysterious laboratory equipment could give the impression that something sinister is going on, and so agitate the bowel.

Equipment can act as a territorial marker. Outsiders visiting the area will be impressed by arcane and potentially dangerous apparatus and feel that they are trespassing. This effect can be exploited by deliberately leaving equipment lying around in an apparently careless way. Interestingly, a hi-fi system is often one of the first things to be introduced into a new dwelling by a young male. Expensive and powerful-looking modules connected by various wires come to dominate the bedsit. Perhaps he fancies that the equipment advertises his wealth and discrimination to other males. He might also harbour the (almost certainly flawed) belief that the equipment makes him more sexually attractive.

Perhaps *Wired-Up B.S.* evolved to help us recognise territory belonging to someone or something else (see also *Trespass B.S.*). It could stop us from entering the lair of a hostile intelligence. Equipment left lying around certainly suggests that an intelligence has been at work and has not bothered to conceal its presence.

Wired-Up B.S. could also help us to recognise a trap. A spider's web is an example of a trap that looks like draped wires.

However, *Wired-Up B.S.* is not a simple warning device, for other types of B.S. are present too. Wires and other devices that are strewn about modify our reaction to a place. They indicate different features and highlight unexpected relationships between the points that they connect. As the eye follows the wires, so it scans the room in a novel way. Attention is paid to details that might normally be overlooked. The wires emphasise volumes in the same way that overhead cables and aeroplane vapour trails give scale and perspective to the sky. They are trajectories made visible. As the wires criss-cross each other, they create delicate, complex frames stretched across empty space. It is as if the location had been prepared for a detailed inspection (see *Investigation B.S.*). Some of these cables might disappear through walls or burrow beneath floorboards and so generate a potent *Partition Penetrating B.S.*

As well as accentuating unusual links, wires and equipment contrast strongly with their surroundings, with their metal and plastic set against earth, cement, carpet, wood, brick, or rock.

Places bestrewn with equipment might provoke a child-like curiosity. The urge to investigate feels naughty, and this gives a thrill to the bowel.

Teleportation

Teleportation is the ultimate in telecommunication and so triggers an excruciating B.S. It is a potent fictional device in which real objects can be sent just like information. Extraordinary journeys can be imagined that take the traveller further from home than would otherwise be possible. It is also a perfect escape mechanism, so people can visit places that would ordinarily be too risky to contemplate.

POSTAL SYSTEM B.S.

The postal system carries millions of items around the world. As a reliable and all-embracing network—almost omnipresent—it feels nearly abstract. Post is similar to, but slower than, electronic telecommunications and is B.S. for similar reasons (including that it connects everyone to the herd; see *Network B.S.*). However, the post can transport real objects, not just information. It is a global network of routes for (usually) inanimate things (see also *Emissary Machine B.S.*).

Post Offices

Post offices are the stations of the huge and dynamic postal system—reliable and predictable places through which a great deal of traffic passes (see *Station B.S.*). They are concrete compared to the abstract postal system and quite stationary, whereas the mail is in transit. This sets up a huge *B.S. Tension*.

Postal Items

Letters and parcels can be aimed with incredible accuracy to almost any location in the world simply by writing the address on them. They enter the extraordinary currents of the postal system that carry them wherever they ask to go. It is very B.S. to think about fragile things like pieces of paper making this journey all by themselves.

Mail Order Businesses

Nowadays, businesses can run from tiny offices, advertising and delivering almost exclusively through the mail (with the occasional use of the telephone and fax). The customer will probably never meet the vendor. The postal system is the virtual shop. Even payment is made by post (or occasionally by telephone or fax, in the case of credit card transactions).

Mailing lists and customer lists are stored on a computer. Such databases are models of that business's commercial world. Browsing the customer database would feel like following the goods to their destinations. The customer database is a directory of where the products have ended up. How B.S. if those goods were videos that contained images of the operator's own house and family!

Such an operator could, by use of mail order, insert his personal images into libraries and institutions around the world (see *Emissary Machine B.S.*).

The mail-shot, in which many potential customers are sent advertising material, is very B.S. It can be done from the office or from home. In monumental selling drives, less turmoil occurs if everything is printed from lists stored on a computer. Letters fan out across whole continents and in some cases all around the world. Replies then arrive like faint echoes from the call. The mail-shot is like a slow-acting radar scanning unknown territory (see *Probe B.S.*).

The B.S. of a mail order business can be dramatically increased if it operates from a distant post office box. The box becomes a remote annex to the office, supplied with a door and key, just like a real room. As if this were not enough, the box straddles the wall of a general post office and so generates *Partition Penetrating B.S.* Visiting the box (especially at night) is like stopping off at a refuge that is too small to climb into, which creates *False Refuge B.S.* Opening the box on a cold night, one might be lucky enough to get a blast of warm air from the post office.

The products in stock are like travellers patiently awaiting their passage, their destinations being decided when the orders arrive.

Stamps & Stamp Collecting

Stamps clearly carry the identity of the country of origin. This can give a foreign letter a very exotic feel. Within a country, stamps may have a unifying and reassuring effect on senders and recipients of mail (see *Network B.S.*). The Queen's head might remind the British of their monarchy. Media of all kinds use this technique. Video graphics that introduce television programmes, or the mastheads of newspapers, use such a repetition of august images.

In icons of this kind, there is a contrast between the design (as an abstract and incorruptible thing) and the unique fate of each copy of the image (which is a particular thing that is real and corruptible). The masthead of a newspaper remains undamaged as an idea, but a copy on newsprint will be degraded and discarded. A corporate logo may be a shining and wonderful thing in the minds of executives, but copies of it sent out on envelopes will be thrown in the rubbish bin almost as soon as the letter has been opened. This creates a type of B.S. called *Abstract–Particular B.S.* This wide scattering of copies, most of which perish, is reminiscent of a spawning, in which millions of offspring are discharged in the hope that a few will survive.

The small but beautifully executed pictures on stamps go all over the world. It is B.S. to think about pictures being so well-travelled, especially when they are on the outside of letters or packages. Stamps seem exquisitely fragile, yet they survive great journeys.

Collecting stamps allows you to pull together small, well-travelled items, which you can inspect in fine detail. Different designs make it easy to date stamps and place them in categories, such as country of origin or subject illustrated, which generates *Collection B.S.*

Maps

Maps are B.S. because they show the layout of land and recall the patterns observed by early B.S. Man. They might show escape routes, safe places, and even the position and movement of enemies and predators. Poring over a map is like taking a virtual trip across the land. Knowing that this is done in complete safety generates a form of *Remote Control B.S.* Maps give the impression of containing and controlling a territory. Possession of the map is possession of the land: a brand of sympathetic magic. Plans of buildings and the designs of ships and spacecraft are B.S. for the same reason. In these cases, the B.S. might be a warning against thinking that the map really does give power over the land.

Models of pieces of land are B.S. for the same reason. Architectural models, or the wonderfully detailed landscapes used in model railways, can stir up a frisson.

The B.S. & Collecting

Collecting and classifying items gives a sense of power and security. A comprehensive and structured collection gives an overview of a system in the way that a map gives an overview of territory. Collections may highlight links between distant items—for example, a chronological sequence of artefacts or a collection of stamps from different periods and countries. A collection shows connections like a map shows routes.

Drug B.S.

TAKING DRUGS may furnish an excuse to inspect B.S. things or visit B.S. places. Under normal circumstances, such activities would seem foolish or suspicious.

A smoker can stand outside an office block and watch the world go by, or contemplate the night from a front garden or balcony, without attracting attention. If the person were not smoking, these activities would look very strange. Smoking also gives an excuse to spend time doing apparently useless things. Having a smoke is understandable, whereas looking at the pavement or the silhouette of a tree for ten minutes is generally frowned upon. The exaggerated expressions of approval that cross the smoker's face during inhalation and the look of bliss afterwards can mask any expressions of appreciation of the environment. A non-smoking B.S. connoisseur pulling similar faces while observing the details of the world would be thought mad.

With a beer in hand, many peculiar objects that would be dismissed as inconsequential in normal life can be examined slowly and thoughtfully. Indeed, whilst drinking, something as apparently uninspiring as the pattern of grooves and stains on a table can become a fascinating landscape.

People may congregate to use and share drugs in the most inhospitable places: multi-storey car parks, under bridges, by canals, in bus stations and in public parks at night. They might believe that their choice of an uncomfortable location is a rational way of avoiding detection or a statement of rejection of middle-aged comforts.

Psychotropic drugs might induce a trance that helps to awaken primitive perceptions, including the B.S. (the effect is complicated, since drugs could also dim the perception of danger). A person taking hallucinogenic drugs might see surreal and unexpected combinations of objects. These drug-induced ideas could then be incorporated into art or fiction. Those that are B.S. might lodge in the memory better and so survive beyond the haze. In other words, the drug causes the person to create unusual images, some of which are promoted because they are B.S.

The combination of trance, heightened sensitivity, the risk of prosecution, a dangerous location, and a reduced awareness of threat, might conspire to make a drug-taking experience compelling. The delicious bowel-tingling sensation of doing something illicit might be a very important component of addiction.

This is not to say that drug-taking is motivated by the B.S., but rather that an unrecognised B.S. thrill is one element in the complex amalgam of addiction. Some people may even use drugs to mask B.S. behaviour. Imagine the difficulty that an inarticulate and shy youngster would have in explaining the B.S. to an unsympathetic peer group.

Crime B.S.

IT MAY BE THAT THE URGE of some burglars to deface rooms with excreta originates in a combination of *Empty Building B.S.* and *Trespass B.S.* Lacking insight into the B.S. and unable to generate it in any other way, they are driven to repeat the crime to recapture the elusive visceral experience. With each new break-in, the sensation grows stronger until they are addicted to the crime without knowing why. Perhaps the prospect of being caught and made an outcast from society generates a prospective *Separation from the Herd B.S.*

It would be a strange thing indeed if crimes of trespass were due to the uninitiated trying to B.S. themselves. Another B.S. motivation for crime might be an urge to get into print. The benighted felon is unlikely to make a lasting contribution to the sum of human knowledge, and the only avenue to fame and immortality is as a case history.

The B.S. & Investigation

When a scene is subjected to intense study (such as may occur during a survey, an archaeological dig, or in a forensic investigation), it may yield unexpected and B.S. relationships. Measurements that are not normally taken, or even thought about, are carefully recorded. Samples and objects are removed from the scene and catalogued. Layers may be stripped away. The scene is dissected and its innards laid bare (see *Dissection B.S.*). The underlying anatomy of the place stands in stark contrast to its earlier appearance. The everyday approximations that used to apply to the scene are replaced by an obsessional attention to detail. In the cases of archaeological or forensic reconstructions, histories are teased out from the clues that remain so that past events can be reconstructed.

The threads of the histories knot together at the scene of the investigation, spreading out later as information from the scene is taken away. The scene becomes the point at which the contrast between a series of past events and the subsequent efforts to understand them is focused. The information that has been extracted from the scene may be stored in books or reports lodged in a variety of safe places distant from the original scene. Aspects of the scene may be reconstructed in a museum or a courtroom. These reconstructions, in conjuring up a sense of the scene, make a B.S. connection. The B.S. is made stronger if the results of the investigation are watched by several people (members of a group inspecting the work of an aberrant member).

When a murder is committed in a mundane place, that place becomes scrutinised and so transformed (see *Scene of Crime B.S.*). It is cordoned off and inspected very carefully. The forensic investigation operates on a small scale and in a precise way, whereas the events that it hopes to illuminate were gross (in size and nature) and messy (physically and intellectually).

Subsequently, a court will witness a highly stylised reconstruction of the event. Everything in the courtroom is stolid and safe. From this secure vantage, the assembled company watches a drama—one that is the very opposite of stolid and safe—played out. There is a potent contrast between the calm and structure of the court proceedings and the loose passion of the crime, and between the stolid courtroom and the quotidian crime scene. It is like a play in which the stage (the crime scene) is too offensive to lie within the theatre and so lies remotely, the actions of the players being conveyed by speakers. (Imagine an august company facing backwards in a cinema and critics relaying the action of the film.) It is strange how the events are transformed into something approaching fiction, and it may be that by turning them into a story they become safer and more contained. Things are improved in the retelling, much as personally remembered events become suffused with magic when contemplated in retrospect.

Occasionally, the court goes to the crime scene. This is terribly B.S. The explicit role that everyone has gives the group a structure and security, even when they are away from the courtroom. Any organised group that moves *en masse* to unfamiliar places generates the B.S. They are like a herd that wanders off into unknown pastures. The members huddle together while peering at strange and threatening sights, relying on each other for security and wishing that they were back in their accustomed surroundings.

Beyond the contrasts, there will be a confluence of things, which is always B.S. All sorts of histories will be pertinent to the crime and converge on the scene. The crime is pivotal, sharply dividing the events leading up to it from those flowing from it. The criminal act, the investigation and the trial will each act like a narrow doorway through which must march all kinds of odd characters and events. Each doorway constrains these things to great closeness, which increases the *B.S. Gradient.*

If the crime scene is particularly sordid or banal, then the prominence it achieves will transform it—the commonplace is elevated to art (see *Framing B.S.*). Crimes also agitate us because one of our number has turned predatory. The disturbances to the scene are inspected closely and have a fascination for us. Perhaps a similar interest was evoked in our ancestors when they came across a member of their species that had been killed by another animal.

Time B.S.

THE PAST is a safe and reliable place because it is unchangeable. Nothing can threaten the events of the past, for unexpected attack is impossible. It is a resolved place, whereas the present is still unfolding. The contrast between the definite past and the uncertain present generates a *B.S. Tension*. Anything that suggests the past can therefore elicit the B.S.

By imagining a trip backwards in time, we can short-circuit the immense potential difference between the present and the past. Since the trips are imaginary, there are no real paradoxes; we can have wonderful adventures without meddling in causality. This type of imagined past is really just another secure place that we can visit. Such a visit is really a nostalgic indulgence, with significant overtones of regression into childhood. It is a return to the parental home.

Another type of time travel can be imagined which takes us to unknown and hostile places, where our actions have real consequences. This type of journey does not generate the B.S. by using the contrast between the mutable present and the immutable past. It is B.S. because of the contrast between the relatively safe present and the hazards of an unknown time.

If time travel were possible, then predators might pursue us down another dimension. There would be no hiding place. We would live in a terrifying universe in which secure time machines would be the only refuges.

Many everyday objects suggest past events: old books, furniture, equipment, or pieces of old buildings, for example. If these objects have personal associations, perhaps dating from childhood or adolescence, then the effect is enhanced. Examples include a picture book from our nursery, our desk from junior school, or a model aeroplane or boat that we made in our teens.

In some locations, time seems to stand still and the weight of the years holds everything in place. Attics, and similar places whose contents have lain undisturbed for long periods, are exceedingly B.S. Walking inside feels like travelling backwards in time. Sometimes, this feeling is compounded by a fear of ghosts (see also *Supernatural B.S.*) or other visitations from the past.

Clocks

In marking out the seconds with their ticking, mechanical clocks emphasise the passage of time and elicit *Tem-*

poral B.S. Because they have performed this function in the same way for so long, they seem to connect the past to the present (they were ticking away in the same fashion fifty years ago, for example). Repetitive or periodic actions that give a structure to time are discussed in *Festival B.S.* Some clocks give the impression that they could be used as time machines by turning the hands backwards.

Grandfather clocks have ponderous mechanisms, wooden cabinets and a deep sense of age. The combination of a metal mechanical device and a wooden cabinet is B.S. —think of old radio sets—perhaps because the addition of clockwork to a piece of furniture generates *Motorised B.S.* If the clock stands in a hallway, like a primitive mechanical sentinel, the effect is boosted by proximity to a highly trafficked area. They also look rather like wooden petrol pumps.

Grandfather clocks often have glass at the front so that the pendulum can be seen swinging slowly. It is like having a window in the belly of the machine. This cabinet can also look big enough to climb into, which creates *False Refuge B.S.*

External public clocks at railway stations, in market squares, and those outside banks and offices, are very B.S., especially when they project from a wall (*External Mechanism B.S.*). Imagine flying up to one late on a rainy night and repairing it. Mechanical clocks that are an integral part of a building generate a form of *Motorised*

B.S., since their metal working parts contrast with the brick and stone. Their clockwork might even suggest an engine and so generate *Impeded Vehicle B.S.*, like having an ineffectual outboard motor on a brick boat.

Clocks on the tops of towers (see *Pole B.S.* and *Tower B.S.*) tend to be rather heavy and primitive devices. The monumental buildings that support these clocks look solid and unchanging, yet they often have a view over the hustle and bustle of everyday life. The clocks gaze out impassively, thinking of years, while the townspeople below are concerned with the commerce of the moment. The tower projects above the wash of people like a lone cliff above the tides.

The clock tower in the centre of Leicester is like a small church steeple that has accidentally wandered into the town square. A small arched door suggests that the clock tower might contain rooms that could be used as cramped headquarters. The clock tower is a common meeting place. Double-decker buses constantly grind around it, like steamships around a lighthouse, which creates a potent *Proximity to Traffic B.S.*

Extremely large and ornate timepieces, such as those found inside some churches or cathedrals, with figures that march around, are exquisitely B.S. These devices are somewhat reminiscent of mechanical street organs, and some have trumpeters, bell-ringers, or cymbal players to chime the quarter hours. Such huge and extravagant machines can look like impossible vehicles and so generate *False Vehicle B.S.* and *Indoor Vehicle B.S.*

The B.S. & Festivals

Festivals are special times that contrast sharply with everyday life. They are milestones in time. Those connected with astronomical events seem to transcend everyday life because they are anchored to ancient rhythms beyond the Earth. They are the temporal equivalent of buildings dotted on wild terrain. This similarity to refuges makes festivals B.S. Passing from one festival to another is like dashing from one safe haven to the next, normal days being the exposed ground that lies between the buildings.

These havens are made more cosy by rites and rituals, because repeated actions give a sense of structure and security. Festivals are a sort of compulsive behaviour on the part of the group in the face of eternity.

During a festival there is a strong sense of community spirit and people gather to celebrate. Returning to the bosom of the family and exchanging cards and gifts makes Christmas deeply comforting. There is a heightened sense of kinship with one's fellows. Cuddling up with the rest of the flock adds to the B.S. because there is safety in numbers. With festivals, it is the unplumbable depths of eternity that scare us more than predators, but the principle is the same. For Christmas and other midwinter festivals the effect is amplified by the cold weather and desolation. Everything about Christmas is bright and cheerful, with plenty of noise and light to ward off the misery of mid-winter. This was even more important in the past, when the celebrations shone out like beacons, lighting up the interminable winters. Those who celebrate Christmas in the southern hemisphere are deprived of this contrast between the warmth of the huddled flock and the cold outdoors. Consequently, Australians get an impoverished form of *Festival B.S.* at Christmas. However, those of American or European extraction can enjoy a cold Christmas by proxy when they talk to relatives back home. This is augmented by *Telecommunications B.S.*

There are many bowel-tugging images associated with Christmas:

The chestnut roaster stands alone as the snow falls softly around him, with nothing to warm him but his stove (*Inadequate Machine B.S.*). He interacts periodically with passers-by but remains separated from the general goings-on. The chestnut roaster works while others feed (see *Edge of the Herd B.S.*).

Christmas trees might trigger deep memories of when we lived in trees. Their decorations and lights make them very attractive homes indeed. Bright and cheerful, with presents at their feet, Christmas trees are thrilling to an ape in search of a perfect dwelling. Those in the hall or lounge therefore generate *House within a House B.S.*, while those at the bottom of the garden stand in splendid B.S. isolation.

Father Christmas has more than his fair share of bowel-tumbling attributes. He spends his year in his workshop at the North Pole and only goes out after dark on Christmas Eve. He flies through the freezing night in an open sledge, skims the glistening slates of millions of roofs and clambers down chimneys.

It is very B.S. to gaze out from the celebrations into the cold and ignored exterior. In fiction, characters may celebrate Christmas when they are lost in some inhospitable place. A sense of normality is preserved, even in the face of danger and the unknown. This feeling can be evoked by imagining pressing your nose against the window and looking out across the snowscape while behind you Christmas dinner is served. Equally, you might imagine wandering off around the house, looking into the cellar or attic, to enjoy the delicious sensation of being alone and exposed while everyone else is together feasting and enjoying themselves. This is the modern equivalent of standing on the fringes of the herd, looking about anxiously for predators, while those in the interior of the group browse unconcernedly. A very steep *B.S. Gradient* runs across the peripheral individual, for behind is the safety offered by others of the species, while in front lies exposure. This may explain the perverse urge to go off and do something useful while everyone else is having a party. By acting as a sentinel—aware and functional while everyone else vegetates—you automatically elicit *Edge of the Herd B.S.*

When we contemplate our short life spans, lost in the vastness of eternity, it is comforting to believe that our festivals will continue forever. For example, it would be reassuring to think that Christmas Day will be celebrated long after we are dead.

Christmas is closely linked with the turn of the year and so it emphasises the unknown year stretching ahead. We look out from the warm lounge-room of Christmas into the cold street of the New Year. In this respect, Christmas is rather like a super-weekend. A weekend is a comfortable retreat before the uncertainties of work, and this weekend effect colours the other five days. Monday is barren—in at the deep end. Tuesday hangs adrift (B.S.). Wednesday is firmly in the middle, like an island. Thursday approaches the weekend but is separated from it (B.S.). Friday nestles against Saturday and gains comfort from it (B.S.). Each day has its own special B.S. flavour, and so events can be made more or less B.S. depending on which day of the week they occur. Being sensitive to the subtle differences in the days of the week can help you construct a more effective *B.S. Fantasy*. The hours of the day, too, have varying B.S. flavours, and carefully choosing the hour, day, and season for a *B.S. Fantasy* can improve its effectiveness.

In conclusion, the fixed timing of a festival and its associated rituals give it a structure like a building, while the

communal acts of celebration fill that building with people. Festivals are thus like crowded houses, full of life, in
the middle of stretches of cold and deserted time. They
are even more potent for being unrecognised as such and
—firmly embedded in time—they also invoke various
types of *Temporal B.S.*

Astronomical B.S.

CONTEMPLATING THE STARS can be very B.S. because it is the ultimate form of looking outside. On a clear night, nothing seems to lie between us and the rest of the universe. The effect is enhanced if there is a refuge nearby, which is why an image of a small house against a starry night is so moving. The house is like a balcony sticking out into space.

If you imagine looking down into the night sky rather than up, then the heavens become a deep, clear sea, full of sparkling life. This makes them terrifying because we fear things in the ocean (*Proximity to Water B.S.*). The thought that we are hanging from the underside of the planet over infinity is quite unsettling: we might drop off and fall into space forever. There is an urge to run for cover.

It is sobering to think that we are made of recycled star matter—like looking at the ocean and wondering about our fishy roots. The thought of stars converting into people disturbs our bowels and forms one extreme of *Re-Cycling B.S.* (the other end of the spectrum contains objects carved out of driftwood).

Professional astronomy seems a B.S. undertaking to me. Collecting data in distant and isolated observatories, reducing the data using machines in lonely offices, and all the while knowing that what is being modelled is mind-bendingly far away. Looking at the stars while everybody else is happily getting on with their Earth-bound duties generates a potent *Egregious B.S.* Peering beyond the edge always does.

The search for extra-terrestrial intelligence is the ultimate in *Probe B.S.* Sending messages into space and waiting for a reply evokes a kind of cosmic *Telecommunications B.S.* Attempting to detect patterns in incoming data reflects the basic B.S. process of sensing other life-forms by the nearly invisible impressions they make on the environment.

More dangerous and B.S. than simply scanning for aliens is sending out messages to them. Hailing unknown life-forms is like advertising to potential adversaries. Standing on the edge of the herd and scanning the night for predators is one thing; calling out to them is quite another.

Attempting to contact aliens is like hunting for distant stations on an old radio. It is hard to know where to turn the dial, and our detectors seem more primitive than any technology the aliens might have.

The B.S. & Space Travel

The natural extension of studying the planets and stars through telescopes is to visit them. This can be done by probes (see *Probe B.S.* and *Remote Control B.S.*) and by manned spaceflight. Setting off on such long and hazardous journeys generates a *Travelling B.S.* of truly heroic proportions. Space travel is the most extreme form of leaving the herd imaginable and would therefore generate massive waves of *Leaving the Herd B.S.* On top of this, the spacecraft themselves agitate the bowel because they are small refuges in the hard vacuum of space. Contact with the control room on Earth would trigger *Telecommunications B.S.*, while spacewalks connected to the ship by a lifeline generate *Umbilical B.S.*

I certainly found the Apollo missions to the Moon intensely B.S., but I was too young to understand why. Now the explanation seems more obvious: the shedding of stages by the rocket created *One Way Vehicle B.S.* Leaving the mother ship in orbit around the Moon, landing in a separate craft, then exploring in a moon buggy created a *B.S. Cascade* of space vehicles. Leaving part of the landing craft on the surface of the Moon generated *Parachute B.S.* The landing craft itself looked like a small metal hut on legs and so generated *Pole B.S.* As if this were not enough, I remember that the astronauts had to sleep when they arrived rather than get out and explore, which provoked appalling *Turnabout B.S.*

Supernatural B.S.

FEAR OF THE SUPERNATURAL is ancient and can provoke gut-rending B.S. This is only to be expected, since hostile supernatural beings are, in effect, super-predators. These days, super-predators are more commonly chosen from science fiction. Aliens have largely usurped ghouls, although vampires and zombies are still with us. Sitting in a haunted house in a motorised chair, or skimming through a deserted. graveyard on a flying pogo stick, would excite waves of B.S.

Supernatural entities have several advantages over natural ones when incorporated into a *B.S. Fantasy*.

First, their strengths and abilities are unknown, so it is difficult to judge how safe a refuge is from them. A sanctuary capable of keeping out people might be virtually transparent to a ghost or be pushed aside by a zombie. This gives all refuges a sense of fragility, triggering *Unreliable Refuge B.S.*, which acts as a warning that the refuge can suddenly fail to offer protection. Imagine cowering in a telephone box hoping to avoid the undead as they wander past.

Second, their powers of pursuit are probably well developed. If a refuge cannot be found, or if one fails, then running away is the only option. This often involves a vehicle, and so reliance is placed on a machine. In horror stories, these machines often underperform, generating *Impeded Vehicle B.S.* Supernatural entities might also exert control over machinery, and so disable even the most robust vehicles.

Third, the range of weapons against them is limited, and the value of such weapons is doubtful. Conventional weapons are probably ineffective and may themselves be disabled by supernatural forces. This generates *Unreliable Machine B.S.* and *Inadequate Machine B.S.* Occult techniques are the only way to deal with supernatural threats because scientific methods are out of their depth. Magic is not a sure-fire thing, so using it puts the person out on a limb, like relying on a weapon that might be a sham. Religious faith is also an option. Horror stories tend to play on faltering faith, pitching a priest, or similar figure, against a demon with nothing to protect him but his weakened belief in his god. Devices against supernatural threats include crucifixes that may or may not halt the advances of a vampire, and spells to ward off demons. Amulets can be regarded as supernatural unreliable machines, and their operation may generate *Out on a Limb B.S.*

Old buildings with an atmosphere of decrepitude can stir the bowels. There is a constant urge to run out of them, a sense of trespassing in a lair. The dishevelled appearance suggests that what lives there is a kind of monster. Lingering in an empty and unloved house generates a delicious sense of mischief. Imagine camping for the night in the far bedroom of an unfurnished house that has been on the market for a year. If something stirred in the night, you would have to walk the full length of the corridor and down the stairs to reach the front door—passing several empty rooms on the way. A haunted house evokes *Empty Building B.S.*, *Trespass B.S.* and *Supernatural B.S.*

Being pursued by horrors seems rooted in sex, and sexual pursuit seems to contain elements of predation. The clever amalgam of death and desire in vampirism is reminiscent of venereal disease, but it also seems to have another deep echo in the psyche, for when something is lethal, it exerts a strange magnetism. There is a certain sensuality in submitting to the predator. It may simply be too exhausting to fight the danger, making it preferable to walk straight into its arms. This may be a form of death wish, but it might also be a latent mechanism allowing sexual submission. Perhaps seduction is linked with predation because insemination leads to pregnancy, which is the most sophisticated form of parasitism.

Supernatural predators are usually human-like, with a few distinguishing qualities, and so are more likely to elicit a sexual submission response than members of another species. Indeed, the nightmare urge to give up the struggle to escape and simply walk toward the very source of one's fear seems to be elicited only by supernatural predators.

Constructed or unleashed monsters have been very popular in fiction because they provide an excellent excuse for having a super-predator wandering about. The idea of a product attacking its producer is unsettling, to say the least, and is linked with various types of *Machine B.S.*

It may be that part of the attraction of horror stories lies in their ability to excite the B.S. Gothic ingredients such as huge dark houses, storms, mysterious figures, and an air of psychological malice certainly spice things up.

THE B.S. & HIDDEN POWER

Concealed human abilities can also generate the B.S. Such hidden (or occult) powers may be dreamed of by anyone who is exposed and defenceless in the face of danger. An unarmed person surrounded by thugs in a dark alley might wish for the powers of a superhero. The ability to fly, or to stun an opponent using special rays, would remove the danger. Abilities that are more psychic would also come in handy, such as the power to induce vomiting or agonising pain in an opponent simply by staring (a version of the evil eye), or the ability to toss people around like rag dolls using psychokinesis. Such abilities might also be turned inward to generate frightening theatrical effects. A threatened person might fantasise about the ability to levitate, to make his skin glow, or to generate thunderous voices. These skills would make the attackers think that their victim possessed supernatural, or even demonic, powers.

Covert powers are often employed in B.S. fantasies and other works of fiction (presumably unknowingly). Hidden and apparently impossible powers are highly protective. They form an invisible armour, a protective bubble that moves with the person, a backpack refuge. A storyteller who uses the device of concealed powers can take characters into regions that it would be foolhardy to visit under normal circumstances. The audience is aware of the powers that lie dormant and can therefore accept the apparent stupidity of the actions. Entering into the spirit of the story, the audience feels the delicious thrill of toying with danger. In such fiction, a person could wander around the most unsavoury districts at night or explore the surface of a hostile planet (see also *Remote Control B.S.* for a discussion of entering hostile places by proxy).

There is always the danger that concealed powers might fail (being mechanical, psychic, or supernatural, they would be unreliable). This creates an additional species of B.S. related to *Unreliable Machine B.S.* Mechanical devices that might fail include a concealed weapon that jams or a teleportation device that stops working. Psychic powers are notoriously unreliable, mysterious, and hard to quantify, and they may fail because of stress. Supernatural powers might require a ritual to evoke them, and there is the fear that the ritual would be performed wrongly, or take too long (see *Task B.S.*).

As well as psychic abilities, equipment that disguises its power can be very B.S. A small and decrepit old car with an extremely powerful new engine would have this effect. So would an old radio set or music cabinet fitted with the latest hi-fi technology, or a tumble-down shed that contained a supercomputer (see also *Furniture in Contrast with its Surroundings*). *Hidden Power B.S.* is partly due to the obvious contrast between the outer casing and the internal mechanism.

Knowing that a character in a dangerous place has hidden powers is like knowing about a hidden escape route —and detecting hidden escape routes lies at the core of the B.S.

ART B.S.

UNDERSTANDING THE B.S. gives insight into modern art and explains the success of certain works. Next time you wander through a gallery showing inexplicable pieces with no apparent merit, pause to consider their B.S. qualities. Perhaps the B.S. explains why such items as misplaced kitchen appliances, modified chairs, and piles of rocks are so respected.

Much conceptual art is B.S. and seems designed to illuminate hidden or abstract relationships. Surrealist work is often B.S., bringing together disparate things and calling into question normal assumptions about everyday objects.

Constructions in galleries are especially B.S., being fragile and incongruous assemblages positioned near public thoroughfares (*Proximity to Traffic B.S.*). Before being transported to the next venue, they may have to be carefully dismantled, with the constituent parts labelled and packaged to ensure that they can be properly reconstituted later. The perverse amount of work involved triggers *Task B.S.*, and the effort of dismantling, packaging, transporting, and rebuilding becomes integral to the artwork itself. There is a parallel with the dismantling and transportation of buildings. Imagine the B.S. of numbering all the bricks to ensure that the structure could be rebuilt when it arrives at its new location, perhaps thousands of miles away (see *Temporary Structure B.S.*).

Framing an object for exhibition emphasises and protects it and so generates *Framing B.S.* Found objects and assemblages displayed in galleries are powerful examples of this. It is surprising how much modern art relies on transforming the everyday into a permanent exhibit. The collection and display of ephemera is the quintessential expression of this type of *B.S. Transformation*. It is not imperative to display framed objects in a gallery, since they can be framed *in situ* and turned into B.S. works of art. An old light switch in someone's cellar could be lovingly framed in gilded wood. A sheet of glass in front of the switch would stop visitors from playing with it. The framed switch could be illuminated internally and have a name tag attached beneath the frame. This tag might contain information about the designer of the switch, where it was made, the name of the person who originally fitted it, the succession of owners of the property, and finally the date on which the switch became a B.S. artwork. Simple framing is sufficient for exposed objects, but dissection is needed before hidden objects can be displayed. Thus, the B.S. artist might wish to demonstrate the fabulous qualities of the space beneath his floorboards. To do this, he might cut an oblong hole in the floorboards of the upstairs landing of his terraced house. The space could be lit by bulbs fitted to the joists. The missing section of floor would then be glazed and framed. Visitors would be invited to look into the artist's floor and see the cables and pipes quietly going about their business (see *Dissection B.S.*). Framing—and dissection followed by framing—emphasises the richness of everyday objects and highlights their details, one central feature of the B.S. being its ability to sharpen the senses. This is common at historic sites, where partial excavations expose features and display them behind glass. The difference is that everyday objects are rarely thought worthy of such attention. This kind of *B.S. Art* is an archaeology of the present.

Galleries themselves are B.S. because they take things from their natural environment and exhibit them in public. Mysterious objects may stand on plinths (*Pole B.S.*) in the middle of the gallery (*Proximity to Traffic B.S.*), and their only merit is to agitate the bowel. When an object that is normally ignored is put on display, people pay attention to it. They gaze at it afresh and inspect its details. One could, for example, take a small section of wall and floor from the base of a door frame, put it in a glass box, and stand it on a pedestal in a gallery. Visitors could inspect the pile of the carpet, the ends of floorboards and joists, the cracks where the doorframe meets the skirting board, and the trapped dust—without having to adopt the *B.S. Posture*. Such a piece of art would be more B.S. than the same section of door frame *in situ* because it has been dissected, separated from the house, and transported to a public venue. Separated, preserved, observed, and useless, it is pure *B.S. Art*.

Isolated and framed objects need not be displayed before an audience. It is more perverse, and more B.S., to go to all the trouble of preparing the object and then keeping it hidden. Such works might be stored in a gallery but kept out of sight in a small adjoining room. This would provoke *Turnabout B.S.* by proxy in the artist. Lovingly created but concealed works would also generate *Disappointed Structure B.S.*, because they are condemned to an inferior location. Beautifully rendered hidden works might resonate with *Hidden Power B.S.*, because they have great artistic merit and iconic power but are locked away.

Some modern works mimic real objects but are constructed in such a way—or from such inappropriate materials—that they cannot perform their normal functions. The B.S. arises from the contrast between the art object and the class of objects it imitates. A chair that cannot be sat on or a car that cannot move are examples. The technique inverts expectation, creating a special *Contradictory B.S.* Further *B.S. Tension* is generated by the urge to quit the defective object. Perched on an uncomfortable chair, the sitter is torn between standing up and remaining uncomfortable. Similarly, seated in a car that cannot go, one must eventually decide to get out (see *False Vehicle B.S.*).

It is impossible to know whether artists who produce teetering and spindly sculptures, modified chairs, or quirky assemblages are consciously aware of the bowel stirring qualities of their work. When a B.S. arrangement appears during the design process it may send a shiver of pleasure through the creator's bowel, and the arrangement will be favoured. The designer will ascribe this twinge to artistic sensitivity. Critics and consumers will respond to the B.S. features without knowing why, and the artwork will grip everyone. A quiet conspiracy will hold all the parties in its sway and allow the B.S. artwork to succeed.

Art, with all its freedoms, provides the perfect crucible for investigating the B.S., since artists can produce strange things without having to justify them. It would be a fascinating experiment to mount an exhibition of artworks that cynically exploit B.S. principles in order to test these ideas directly.

The B.S. & Subliminal Persuasion

The B.S. usually operates at an unconscious level and is therefore a suitable tool for subliminal persuasion. It is tempting to think it is used in media of all kinds. An amusing and instructive exercise would be to keep track of strange architectural arrangements, exuberant open-plan offices, converted factories, oddly placed chairs, hanging settees, bizarre vehicles, deserted buildings, and surreal juxtapositions in films, television and print. Remember that the B.S. is not obvious, but lies in the general arrangement of things, the overall design, and the positioning of certain details.

The B.S. hooks audiences. The work stimulates our guts and we become fascinated without knowing why. We feel connected to the film, book, play, or television programme at a deep level. It provokes us, and our fascination turns into revenue.

Even if someone suspected that the B.S. were being used as a weapon, as a tool of mass persuasion, or simply as a sales technique, embarrassment about bowel functions would usually prevent an open accusation. However, linking the B.S. to the detection and evasion of predators makes it a more acceptable challenge. As an ancient survival device, the B.S. sits neatly between sex and death, those two famous components of our psyche that are often cynically manipulated.

It could be argued that films are often concerned with fear and that the B.S. is nothing more than a new name for the subtle techniques of tension building. Perhaps the Gothic sets, carefully written music, weapons left lying around, and other cinematic tricks have nothing to do with the B.S. But I prefer to think that it is the other way around: that the tricks work because they tap into the same reservoir of ancient dreads. If you still feel sceptical, keep an open mind the next time you watch a film or music video. Look for the less obvious arrangements. Once you have read this book, you will be amazed at how often the B.S. figures in motion pictures.

The B.S. Trance

During the B.S., we retreat into a private and imaginary safe haven. The *B.S. Fantasy* induces a mild trance that allows us to enter this inner sanctum—a form of self-hypnosis. Reading a story has a similar hypnotic effect, which might explain why people take books and magazines into the toilet.

B.S. Posture

A BIZARRE and faintly embarrassing posture can induce the B.S. Kneel on the floor and stretch forward, supporting yourself on your elbows. Splay your elbows apart so that your chin is near the ground, cupped in your hands. In this position, your belly hangs relaxed and details at ground level can be closely examined. Apart from inducing physical relaxation, the *B.S. Posture* gives a child's eye view of things.

B.S. Sex

LIKE THE B.S., sexual arousal may require a trance-like state. Defaecation and coitus increase vulnerability to attack, and many animals seek a refuge in which to mate. Sexual fantasies certainly have parallels with B.S. fantasies, including a reliance on fine details and the juxtaposition of contrasting elements. However, these similarities may have more to do with the need to create a convincing fantasy than with anything specifically visceral or sexual.

Conclusion

THIS BOOK HAS EXPLORED those thoughts and arrangements that have laxative properties. Such *Bowel Stirring Things* come in all shapes and sizes. They crop up in the most unexpected places and challenge us during our most complacent moments.

In some respects, the bowel stirring response is quite subtle. Someone who experiences it is not scared, but in a state of mild agitation and heightened awareness. The visceral agitation spices things up, much as chilli improves the taste of food through pain, while the heightened awareness increases the range of experiences. This combination is thrilling and profound. The things that trigger the B.S. are not frightening; indeed, they are usually so mundane and innocent that most people ignore them. An appreciation of the B.S. can make these commonplaces extraordinary and help us to see arrangements and qualities that others miss. The process also works in reverse: by concentrating on subtle or embedded patterns, or by creating new ones, one may induce *Connection B.S.* This explains why contemplating historical links or surreal relationships is so bowel tumbling.

The B.S. can be understood and discussed at an intellectual level, but this gives little indication of its true force. At its most basic, it is a powerful and revolting reaction. Its primal force is only appreciated when a full-blown *B.S. Attack* strikes. When this happens, it is impossible to think about anything else. There is no room for artistic contemplation or sophisticated argument, for the whole body is racked by waves of urgency. In this state, virtually any sight or thought makes matters worse. Everything becomes bowel stirring, and it is impossible to concentrate on anything except finding a toilet. If you experience such a reaction, you will be left in no doubt about the reality of the B.S.

Genteel sensitivity on the one hand, and violent incontinence on the other, are just extremes of a continuum. As we scan this bizarre spectrum, we notice one constant: the sharpening of our awareness. When bowel stirred, we see with a terrible clarity. This ability to detect patterns lies at the very heart of the B.S. and strongly suggests that it is a survival mechanism of some kind. Throughout this book, I have argued that the sensation originally developed to protect us from predators. As civilisation has progressed, and predators have become less of a threat, the mechanism has been available for new and more cultural applications. It is like a great engine that is no longer needed for traction and is now free to power recreational machines. The strength of the *B.S. Theory* lies in its ability to unify many attitudes, behaviours, artworks, and commentaries, and to tie them to this biological mechanism.

One of the challenges in writing this book has been to resolve the various *Bowel Stirring Things* into their predatory components. At first, I found this quite difficult and my attempts often seemed contrived. With practice, it became easier. Eventually, it was possible to describe them all in these terms. From a chair in a doorway to an abandoned ship, they all succumbed to the same analysis. The various types of B.S., as defined in the glossary, make up a toolkit that can be used to dismantle artworks and commentaries into their biological components. The insights that *B.S. Theory* provides can also help us to construct ideas and artworks that are novel and compelling.

Many things about the B.S. involve perverse and useless behaviour. This is most evident in *Turnabout B.S.* The agitation may arise from a sensation of lost opportunities, like an intensified version of the feeling we get when we miss a train or sit an exam for which we have failed to study. These feelings can be overwhelming and might explain why some people court failure. Other useless activities may be a way of hiding from insurmountable problems. Strange and repetitive behaviours can emerge in the face of disasters and may generate a sense of security. Recognising these activities in others, or engaging in them ourselves, implies the existence of a serious threat, and it is this allusion to danger that turns our guts. Observing someone performing an odd task in an unusual location may therefore be bowel stirring not just because of *Task B.S.*, but because we recognise the perverse activity as a sign of danger.

To summarise, the bowel stirring feeling, weak or strong, is an archaic warning that something is amiss. If a threat is suspected, if a prospective escape route is blocked, or if a potential refuge is dubious, the twinge in our belly stops us in our tracks and forces us to retreat to safety. If we are already safe, it immobilises us while we think through the risks. At the same time, it helps us to empty our bowels in preparation for a difficult time ahead. The B.S. gives us pause for thought. Because so much has changed over the past few million years, many of the original threats that shaped the B.S. are no longer with us. It is an anachronism, which makes it difficult to understand today: an old vessel, beached on a modern shore. Configured for an ancient world, it can be activated by modern arrangements that recall prehistoric threats. Such modern situations can look harmless but resonate with ancient forms. By interpreting the bowel stirring response in terms of fear and survival, we can begin to understand its symbolism and appreciate its richness and power.

Although apparently ancient, the B.S. is still capable of evolving and being put to creative use. It is a formidable tool that can be applied to all kinds of modern situations. It can help us analyse the actions of others and enrich our own productions. If it really exists, then perhaps other unlikely and exotic mechanisms lie buried in our minds. Such mental equipment might help us dissect reality in novel and entertaining ways. Perhaps we contain a whole range of fossil survival devices that could find novel applications. Maybe they could be discovered by examining how art is produced.

Hopefully, the empty rooms, dark passageways, and disabled vehicles encountered in this book will encourage you to further explore the uncomfortable landscape of the B.S., probe its possibilities, and discuss its merits with family and friends. The young are most likely to be sympathetic to these arguments, for although we are all born with the faculty, its power diminishes with age. Consequently, those over thirty may find the subject unfathomable. However spirited the delivery, it may leave them unmoved. The sad fact is that by the time most people have the insight, courage, and command of language to express their B.S. feelings, those sensations have evaporated and their memory has been suppressed.

Glossary

Abandoned Machine B.S.

Bowel-throbbing discomfiture generated by an abandoned machine. The fear is that the original users have been taken by a predator, and that tarrying near the machine invites a similar fate (see *Empty Vessel B.S.*).

Abstract–Particular B.S.

The B.S. evoked by the contrast between the design of an object and the object itself. The design is an abstract and incorruptible thing, whereas the object is concrete and inhabits the real world where it is prone to damage (see *Outpost B.S.*). Especially strong when multiple objects have the same design. Such things are like members of a species. As individuals, they disperse and suffer various fates, but the design remains intact. The copies are like progeny leaving the parental home, with all the loss of security that implies.

A logo design. Copies of the logo on envelopes, letterheads, vehicles, and buildings. The design of a washing machine and all those individual washing machines that share that design (with particular emphasis on their locations and states of repair). The design and personality of a cartoon character and all the images and models of that character, including those on and in cereal boxes.

Allotments

Extremely B.S. pieces of land that are rented or owned for the purpose of growing vegetables. They are *Distant Gardens* and so are more exposed than gardens adjoining houses. They are made exquisitely B.S. by the presence of a small lockable shed.

Fields of allotments are a nearly perfect example of a *landscape of potential toilets.*

Anchored B.S.

B.S. caused by having something anchored to a particular place. The object, be it a boat, house, or even a chained cycle, is unable to escape (see *Impeded Vehicle B.S.*). *Anchored B.S.* may arise from a sense of being tethered as bait, like a goat tied up to attract a tiger. Discomfiture might also come from contemplating the connection to an inhospitable region, as in an anchor chain connecting a comfortable houseboat to the tangled and filthy bed of an oily canal.

A mobile home that is plumbed into the mains. A marine buoy anchored near a harbour. An oil rig. A rocket still attached to its tower.

Ark B.S.

An extreme version of *Travelling B.S.* triggered by preparing a vessel to evacuate people (or animals) from a dangerous situation (see *One Way Vehicle B.S.*). The obvious survival implications intensify the effect on the bowel. The vessel might save an individual, family, group, or even a species. A more abstract form of *Ark B.S.* might occur when there is an attempt to save an idea, work of art, or even genetic material (see *Emissary Machine B.S.*).

A helicopter evacuating civilians from a war zone. A raft to escape a flood. A lifeboat escaping from a sinking ship. A spaceship leaving a dying Earth, whose occupants hope to colonise other worlds.

Boundary B.S.

B.S. generated near a major boundary. The boundary can be of almost any kind: land–sea, earth–space, city–country, or even metaphorical. Probably originates in the agitation felt near the edge of the forest when viewing open ground (see *Edge of the Forest B.S.*).

B.S.

Short for *Bowel Stirring*. Refers to the uncomfortable but thrilling feeling of urgency in the bowel that is triggered by various real and imaginary things. Used as an adjective, noun, and verb.

A B.S. room. The B.S. He dawdled in the museum to B.S. himself.

B.S. Art

Art that generates a B.S. response. The effect may be deliberately embedded by an artist who is cynically using B.S. techniques, or it may be an accidental side effect. Artworks with B.S. qualities may succeed because of an unconscious selection process. The creator, critic, curator, and collector may all be responding to subliminal B.S. cues.

B.S. Attack

An uncontrollable urgency triggered by a B.S. thought or sight. This is not a mild twinge of gentle appreciation, but a series of spasms that rack the body. When this happens, it is impossible to think about anything else. Someone experiencing a *B.S. Attack* is caught up in a vicious circle, for the level of awareness is so heightened that everything in the environment seems bowel stirring, which raises sensitivity still further. The unfortunate victim looks around wildly, desperately trying to fix an eye on some bowel-calming vision. This usually fails and the sufferer starts to tremble and sweat, fighting to stay continent. They whimper and babble incoherently before rushing off to a toilet, if one is available, or to the next best thing, if it is not. A violent *B.S. Attack* is a defining moment, and someone who has experienced one will be left in no doubt about the power of the B.S.

B.S. Cascade

A sequence of things of decreasing security (an extension of the comfort–discomfort arrangement). A *B.S. Gradient* runs down the cascade.

Mission control – mother ship – landing craft – surface craft.

B.S. Fantasy

A type of daydream used to stir the bowels. The fantasies may be short stories, but usually they are mental tableaux of objects positioned in B.S. locations with the dreamer present in the scene. B.S. fantasies can be used to amusing effect, since they can be described to another person in whom the B.S. can thus be induced. With time, it is possible to build an extensive armoury of these fantasies.

B.S. Frisson

A tingling thrill of B.S. pleasure. A delicious turbulence in the bowel that is insufficient to provoke a bowel motion.

B.S. Gradient

A change in the level of B.S. across a zone, gap, or structure, comparable to a voltage drop. Severe *B.S. Gradients* are, in themselves, B.S. Powerful gradients run through walls and portals, caused by the steep difference in security between inside and outside.

B.S. Paradox

Many apparent contradictions feature in the B.S. The most fundamental is the paradox of being frightened but relaxed and attentive. Most such paradoxes resolve when viewed in terms of predators, because survival depends on being motivated by fear while remaining relaxed enough to make rational judgements and attentive enough to know what is happening. Paradoxes also emerge because predators and prey use similar mechanisms and strategies in their ongoing struggle. Offence and defence seem intuitively asymmetric, so it feels paradoxical when both use the same strategy, as in disguise or armour.

B.S. Potential

A measure of the apparent security (in terms of *B.S. Theory*) that something offers. An object with a very high *B.S. Potential* appears quite safe (a perfect refuge), whereas one with a very low *B.S. Potential* appears highly threatening (exposed territory or an obvious trap). When objects with different *B.S. Potentials* are linked in some way, a *B.S. Gradient* runs between them. Juxtaposing elements with different *B.S. Potentials* creates a *B.S. Tension*. A person responds to differences in *B.S. Potential* by heading for the more secure place (unless they are perverse and hope to B.S. themselves still further).

B.S. Tension

The dissonance or tension between elements that are juxtaposed in a B.S. fashion. A jarring between components of a design caused by a difference in the *B.S. Potential* of the components, rather than by a design clash.

A B.S. Tension exists between a chair and the tarmac of the road on which it sits. A bookcase and the railway platform on which it stands.

B.S. Theory

A general term encompassing the whole corpus of B.S. knowledge, especially the explanations for the phenomenon. *B.S. Theory* can explain the arcana of modern art and the peculiar images that crop up regularly in films, television plays, and music videos.

B.S. Transformation

Occurs when an object is rendered B.S. (or is made more B.S.) by having modifications done to it, by a change of use, or by being moved to a new location or context. A *B.S. Transformation* can usually be analysed further into other component types of B.S.

An electric iron displayed on a plinth in an art gallery. An old car on a pole in someone's front garden.

Camping B.S.

B.S. generated by camping, both normal and perverse. When camping, small and temporary pieces of private territory are staked out in a larger environment. Cooking on stoves provokes *Task B.S.*, while tents provoke *Temporary Structure B.S.* Camping is usually combined with travel and so there will be a background level of *Travelling B.S. Camping B.S.* is more potent if there is some perverse element involved, such as camping in your own back garden for no good reason, or pitching a tent in the middle of a large museum at night, preferably in the Egyptology section (see *Turnabout B.S.* and *Minimal Camping B.S.*).

Change of Use B.S.

The B.S. that occurs when an object or a building is used for a new and unusual purpose—using something in a way not envisaged by its designer.

A car used as a display cabinet for goods in a shop. A church converted into an office. A windmill converted into a dwelling.

Childhood Perspective B.S.

The bowel churning brought on by a situation that makes a person feel childlike and vulnerable. Easily triggered by large-scale furniture, huge interiors, high windows, and other features that make a place look to an adult as it would to a child. This may be part of the reason why the monumental interiors of cathedrals, power stations, and museums are so B.S.

Collection B.S.

Collecting gives a sense of power and security. A collection shows relationships, like a map shows routes. It also hints at trophies and predator pantries.

Comfort–Discomfort

The *B.S. Tension* created by the difference in comfort, safety, or security between two objects, places, or situations. The prospect of moving to a less comfortable situation brings on the urge to void the bowels.

Connection B.S.

The B.S. induced by contemplating the connections between things. Especially strong when those connections are unlikely or slightly surreal. It works because the B.S. is based on a pattern-recognition system that evolved to detect predators. Nowadays, the ability to detect predators is much less important, but the pattern-recognition equipment remains. When we cast around for unlikely patterns, or look for obscure links between things, we activate this ancient detection device and its associated disturbance of the bowels. Much modern art is concerned with highlighting unusual relationships and so can be analysed in terms of *Connection B.S.* Some conceptual art links things in an apparently perverse or random fashion or uses an arbitrary logic to join objects together. History, too, involves many abstract connections and so can trigger *Connection B.S.*

Contradictory B.S.

The *B.S. Tension* created by the contradiction between the apparent function of an object and the way it is built. The materials used and the method of construction make the object unworkable (see *False Vehicle B.S.* and *False Refuge B.S.*).

A chair made out of nails. A car made out of soft furnishings. A rocket built of matchsticks.

Contrasting Building B.S.

Tension generated when quite different buildings abut one another. Smaller or older buildings might look intimidated by larger ones, or they might offer a refuge on a more personal scale (see *Embedded Building B.S.*).

A small house that survived redevelopment and now stands with an office block on each side. A hut beside a skyscraper. A thatched cottage in the middle of an industrial estate. A very modern glass office wedged into a terrace of small houses with a gas works nearby.

Designer B.S.

Design elements added to give an object B.S. appeal. They may be added intentionally as a cynical exercise, or created unknowingly by the designer. Consumers are attracted to the product without knowing why. Through unconscious feedback from buyer to manufacturer, a runaway B.S. fashion movement might emerge (see *B.S. Art*).

Detail B.S.

B.S. generated by inspecting details, especially architectural ones. It may originate in childhood, when there is a keen interest in the fine surface appearance of things and the most commonplace object is the source of endless fascination. Children prod, poke, and inspect objects from all angles. To them, everything is magical and worth examining.

Adults see the utility, financial value, and prestige of objects but often gloss over their physical appearance. Concentrating on the details and surface appearance can strip back these perceived values and reveal objects in a pristine light. The B.S. restores this clearer, more innocent vision.

The ability of artists to observe the world in this innocent way might explain why so many artworks are B.S.

The B.S. operates by noticing minute shifts in the landscape. Consequently, attention to details has survival value. By concentrating on details, we might activate the underlying mechanism of the bowel stirring response. Details are also more apparent during a B.S. response because of the sensory heightening triggered by the fear of predators.

Diluvian B.S.

B.S. generated by flooding (see also *Proximity to Water B.S.*). It may be a form of *Natural Disaster B.S.*, but probably has a more subtle origin, since the prospect of being swamped by water brings with it the fear of aquatic predators.

Water is more difficult to move through than air and gives a strong sense of impediment—a feeling common in nightmares. Although we might find water difficult, highly adapted aquatic predators, such as sharks, handle the medium with ease. In water, attacks may come from above and below as well as from all sides.

In addition, our visual range is severely limited under water. Vision is even more limited when we are on land trying to peer into water. Consequently, encasing anything in a medium that is physically and optically denser than air can trigger the B.S. This applies to objects contained in solid glass as well as to less obvious cases, such as dense fog enveloping a house.

Submerged buildings are horrifically bowel stirring. Imagine a small village submerged by a reservoir, with only the church steeple protruding above the water. The classical example of a sunken city is Atlantis. Such places also trigger *Empty City B.S.* (at least one hopes they are deserted).

When a town is flooded, everything looks different and its terrestrial vehicles are impeded. See *Framing B.S.* for a discussion of how the presentation of objects alters their B.S. properties. Buildings on poles—designed to withstand floods—are naturally very bowel tugging (see *Pole B.S.*).

Disappointed Structure B.S.

The sense of bowel-aching sympathy evoked by benighted structures. They may look stunted, or mutated, or aberrant, or mutilated, or they may sit in poor locations. Objects that have failed to achieve things in life make us count our blessings—a bowel-tingling *schadenfreude* for unfortunate objects (see also *Liberation B.S.*).

An office window that looks out across an underground car park. A beam engine in a factory that wanted to be a locomotive pulling carriages across the countryside. A chest of drawers kept in a coal cellar when it longs for an airy bedroom.

Dissection B.S.

The B.S. that occurs when the innards of an object are displayed. Unusual exposures of internal structures—as in a partially demolished house or a ripped-open bus—provoke this type of B.S. because they are reminiscent of half-eaten prey.

Dissection-like exposures also reveal latent weaknesses and instabilities. A tumble-down building after an earthquake reveals structural failure. We realise that it was never actually strong enough, and so we feel a shock of retrospective *False Refuge B.S.* A delicious tingle of a near miss.

A bedroom fireplace exposed when a terrace of houses is partially demolished. A roofless shoe-repair and key-cutting booth in a shopping mall. Torn open cars in a scrapyard.

Dissemination of Ideas B.S.

Disseminating ideas creates a subtle form of B.S. As one's ideas go out into the world, they influence others (see *Remote Control B.S.*) and confer a form of immortality (see *Emissary B.S.*). May be linked with procreation.

Writing a book whose copies go everywhere. Making a video that is distributed around the world.

Dissolved Building B.S.

The B.S. that occurs when a private building or room is spread diffusely inside a public one. *Dissolved Building B.S.* is an extreme version of *Embedded Building B.S.*, since the internalised structure is dispersed. An embedded building remains intact as an identifiable bolt-hole, whereas a dissolved one is hard to detect and offers no sanctuary. A dissolved building is a diffuse, leaky, virtual refuge. There appear to be several roots of *Dissolved Building B.S.*: a sense of invasion, exposure, and having been eaten by proxy (a predator having partially digested your room, as in *Incorporation B.S.*). Exploded rooms recall how interiors seemed larger during childhood (see *Childhood Perspective B.S.*). The scattering of objects also suggests strewn wreckage.

Personal shelves scattered in the far corners of a public library. Keeping your television set in an electrical shop surrounded by other televisions, and sitting in the street on a collapsible stool to watch it.

Distant Garden B.S.

Distant gardens are difficult to police and are vulnerable territory (see *Outpost B.S.*). All gardens require tending, which provokes *Task B.S.*, but distant ones are more disturbing because there is no adjacent refuge.

See *Tending the Distant Garden*.

Draining B.S.

Discomfiture felt when contemplating a region that was previously under water but has now been drained. In a sense, it is the opposite of *Diluvian B.S.* Perhaps we fear that the entire stock of aquatic predators is now concentrated in a few remaining puddles, and that they are angry at having had their water drained away.

The ground is likely to be very muddy and covered in tangled weeds and debris, which makes escape very difficult. There may also be elements of *Dissection B.S.*, since the water layer has been stripped back, revealing hitherto sunken structures.

The muddy bed of a lake that has been recently drained, revealing old prams, bedsteads, and fridges dumped over the years. A huge transparent semicircular wall holding back the sea, enabling you to wander far beyond the low-tide mark and see dead sea creatures and shipwrecks. Hovering along drained canals that run through a landscape of derelict factories and warehouses. There would be generations of rubbish littering the floors of the canals, and every so often you would pass a deeply mired barge.

Edge of the Herd B.S.

The sensation elicited when you do something useful (especially sentinel duty) while all around you vegetate. This is the modern equivalent of standing on the fringes of the herd, anxiously scanning for predators, while those in the interior of the group browse unconcernedly. A very steep *B.S. Gradient* exists across the peripheral individual, for behind stands the safety of the herd, while in front lies exposure—the flanking individual becomes a wall.

Egregious B.S.

The type of B.S. caused by standing out from the crowd. Being such a pioneer can give a profound sense of loneliness and exposure. A person with *Egregious B.S.* is on the brink in more than one sense. (See *Boundary B.S., Edge of the Herd B.S.* and *Pioneering B.S.*)

Elevated Chair B.S.

B.S. generated by elevated chairs. Probably a compound of *Pole B.S.*, *Tower B.S.*, *Sitting B.S.*, and *Childhood Perspective B.S.* (raised seats may recall oversized high chairs). Chairs displaced from the floor are disturbing because they are more difficult or dangerous to leave. Consequently, sunken chairs are also highly bowel stirring. A comfortable chair at the foot of cellar steps would be deliciously difficult to sit in.

Lifeguard chairs. An office chair swaying on the top of a pole in a car park. An armchair bolted to the end of a mechanical arm. A wickerwork settee slung from a crane in the middle of a demolition site.

Embedded Building B.S.

B.S. generated by a lesser building (or refuge) inside a greater building (or refuge). Also called *House Within a House B.S.* A *B.S. Gradient* runs across such nested refuges. A series of concentric protective shells around a vulnerable person generates this type of feeling. Children who enjoy building little shelters may experience an early form of this response.

A telephone box in a shopping mall. A newsstand under an arcade. An enclosed booth in an exhibition hall.

Emissary Machine B.S.

B.S. generated by envoy machines that travel alone to perform a task, gather data, or deliver a message or instruction. They are mechanical diplomats. They might carry gene-like instructions and so echo biological reproduction.

Time capsules. Space probes.

Empty Building B.S.

B.S. generated by an empty building. We sense an absent crowd—a feeling that everyone has fled or been eaten. The empty building also offers myriad hiding places for both predator and prey. These dual and opposing roles for hiding places constitute a *B.S. Paradox.*

Wandering around a closed municipal library at night. Sitting on a pew in the middle of a church that has been locked up for the night.

Empty City B.S.

B.S. generated by an empty city or town—an amplified version of *Empty Building B.S.* An empty city is full of potential refuges, but with the danger that they contain enemies.

Empty Room B.S.

B.S. generated by an empty room. Such a room can feel like a part of the outdoors incorporated into the house. The bowels may be stirred because we struggle to explain why the room is deserted. Empty rooms also feel desolate and exposed.

A room being decorated. An unvisited attic.

Empty Vessel B.S.

B.S. generated by a large vessel that is deserted when one expects a crew. A deserted vessel is *emphatically* empty. Even if the vessel were functional, it would be difficult to operate without a crew (see *Impeded Vehicle B.S.*). We suspect that the crew (and passengers) fell prey to something horrible.

A deserted ship in mid-ocean, such as Mary Celeste. A deserted spaceship careering through the vastness of space or crash-landed on a dead planet.

Empty World B.S.

B.S. generated when no one else can be found. The bowel-wrenching fear that you are the last survivor and that whatever killed humanity will get you next. Also called *Post-Holocaust B.S.,* it is an amplified version of *Empty City B.S.* It would also occur when a new planet is colonised.

Venturing forth after a plague or bomb has destroyed civilisation. Colonising a distant planet.

External Mechanism B.S.

B.S. generated by machinery located on the exterior of a building or craft. Such mechanisms are vulnerable to attack, especially if they are vital to survival. External mechanisms may also serve as footholds for invaders. Projecting mechanisms may echo the appendages of ancient predators.

An external winch lifting food supplies to a lofty door in a tower (an invader could block the food supply or climb up). Engines and components slung beneath a motorbike.

False Refuge B.S.

B.S. generated by a place that hints at refuge but is unable to offer accommodation or protection. The space may be too small to climb into, structurally unsound, or illusory. False refuges are distracting and disturbing, and resonant with false hope—like escape vehicles with missing engines (see *Impeded Vehicle B.S.*). They are bewitching and lure you away from real refuges, sidetracking you from escape routes. *False Refuge B.S.* may be a survival mechanism that recognises traps and dead ends. False refuges are attractive partly because we enjoy the *B.S. Frisson* they elicit. They are the *femmes fatales* of the B.S. world.

The cabinet of a grandfather clock that houses the long pendulum looks like an inviting refuge standing in the hallway, but you could not fit inside. A tiny hollow in a wall resembling a cave. An item of furniture which is too cramped to climb into, such as a small chest in a museum.

False Vehicle B.S.

B.S. generated when an immovable object resembles a vehicle. It can also be triggered by permanently disabled vehicles (see *Impeded Vehicle B.S.*). The discomfiture warns us against relying on such objects for escape—for rather than escaping in them, we would be trapped (see also *False Refuge B.S.*).

A windmill resembling a galleon in full sail. A naval building shaped like a ship's superstructure. An observatory resembling a squat rocket. A life-size model vehicle made from inappropriate materials such as matchsticks.

Feeding B.S.

Discomfiture generated when eating or drinking in exposed or unusual places. Eating is preferred in safe, secluded locations; in the wild, feeding in the open would be dangerous. When feeding, your guard is lowered and mobility is reduced (see *Sitting B.S.*). Consequently, restaurants in precarious or perverse locations are highly bowel stirring.

Coffee shops at bus interchanges. Bars at railway stations. Espresso bars inside bookshops or museums.

Festival B.S.

B.S. generated by festivals and celebrations. It may arise because festivals are brief episodes of warmth, comfort, and community enjoyed in the wide bleakness of ordinary time.

Framing B.S.

B.S. generated when an otherwise unremarkable thing has attention drawn to it by a frame or contextual boundary.

A section of floor and skirting board displayed in an aquarium. A found object or piece of ephemera presented as art.

Going Underground B.S.

The B.S. generated by descending into subterranean chambers. Underground rooms, vaults and passageways may be reminiscent of the burrow of some horrifying predator, or they may represent a welcome retreat from the dangers above ground. Underground chambers may also suggest a suitable nest in which to rear young.

The crypt beneath a church. The cellar of a derelict house. Underground trains, platforms and tunnels.

Gothic B.S.

The B.S. generated by Gothic ingredients such as storms, castles and dungeons. There is proximity to elemental forces (see *Lightning Conductor B.S.*) and supernatural beings (see *Supernatural B.S.*).

Haunter B.S.

The B.S. generated by visiting a place but behaving like a ghost. The reluctance to be seen may betray a fear of predators, while the sense of separateness from everyone else generates a potent *Separation from the Herd B.S.* See also *Minimal Camping B.S.* and *Incognito B.S.*

Hidden Power B.S.

The B.S. that occurs when we know about secret powers. A conspiratorial B.S. develops when the author lets us recognise the superhero masquerading as an ordinary person. Hidden powers are highly protective, like invisible armour. Characters with these abilities can venture into regions where it would be dangerous for normal people to go, and the audience gets a delicious sense of toying with danger by proxy (see *Remote Control B.S.*). Equipment of unexpected power can be very B.S. too. Because concealed powers might fail, they also elicit a form of *Unreliable Machine B.S. Hidden Power B.S.* is partly due to the high contrast between the outer casing and the internal mechanism—we feel safer than we look.

Hidden powers are like hidden escape routes, and detecting hidden escape routes is a core activity of the B.S.

A small and decrepit old car fitted with an extremely powerful new engine. An old radio set or music cabinet fitted with the latest hi-fi technology. A tumble-down shed containing a supercomputer.

House within a House B.S.

The B.S. generated by a smaller refuge nested inside a larger one. See *Embedded Building B.S.*

Hybrid B.S.

The B.S. generated by unnatural chimaeras that could turn out to be super-predators. Such unfortunate mutants disturb us partly because we fear what created them. *Hybrid B.S.* can be recognised in many artworks that incorporate disparate elements.

Icarian B.S.

The B.S. generated by daring and flimsy machines. The bowel-tingling hubris felt when constructing, or contemplating using, such dubious home-made devices. Icarian machines are prone to failure and therefore endanger life (see also *Unreliable Machine B.S.*). Named after Icarus, who came to grief after flying too close to the sun on wings held together with wax. As usual, the B.S. acts as a warning.

Home-made flying machines. A rocket assembled in the garden shed. A one-person hovercraft glued and screwed together in the cellar.

Impeded Vehicle B.S.

B.S. generated when a vehicle, or other escape mechanism, is impeded, increasing the risk of capture. Possibly developed as a warning against relying on such machines for escape. It may have roots in childhood experiences of mechanical toy cars, aircraft and spaceships fixed to the ground in shopping malls and out in streets. When coins are inserted, these toys rock and wobble and grind, and wail and beep, and flash their lights in grotesque imitations of trapped robots. Rocking chairs, rocking horses, and swings may also contribute to the childhood genesis of this response. See also *False Vehicle B.S.* and *Inadequate Machine B.S.*

Inadequate Machine B.S.

The B.S. generated by feeble or underpowered devices. Weak machines leave you exposed, for they lack the power to comfort or protect. They tantalise with the promise of safety, but the bowel stirring response warns you not to rely on them. Similar gut-wrenching warnings occur in *False Refuge B.S.*, *False Vehicle B.S.*, *Impeded Vehicle B.S.* and *Refuge-Trap B.S.*

Weak heating devices such as a single-bar electric fire out-doors. Torches emitting a dim yellow glow while exploring a crypt. Poor-quality weapons or armour.

Incognito B.S.

The visceral agitation felt when going incognito. Being cloaked generates a thrill from implied illicit activity, combined with the fear that camouflage is necessary be-cause predators are nearby. See *Haunter B.S., Minimal Camping B.S.* and *Hidden Power B.S.*

Visiting an alien planet disguised as a local. A spy under deep cover in a foreign country.

Incorporation B.S.

The visceral agitation that occurs when something is par-tially or wholly absorbed into something else. The object may be fully immersed, like a fly in amber, or partially embedded, such as a car half-buried in concrete. *Incorpo-ration B.S.* implies entrapment or slow ingestion. A fly wrapped in silk by a spider is the archetypal case. See *Dissolved Building B.S.* and *Wired-Up B.S.*

The façade of an old building incorporated into a modern one. An old boat partially immersed in silt.

Indoor–Outdoor B.S.

B.S. generated when things normally found indoors appear outdoors, and vice versa. Interior objects placed outside emphasise exposure, like furniture in the middle of a road or field. Exterior things like earth, rocks, or trees can be disquieting when inside a building, for they suggest an invasion from the wild.

A bedroom suite in the middle of a field. A cooker and kitchen table on the cracked concrete of a disused airfield. Arrangements of rocks and plants in an office foyer.

Indoor Vehicle B.S.

B.S. generated by placing a vehicle inside a building or otherwise concealing it. Vehicles become especially bowel stirring when kept indoors, since their movement is restricted (see *Impeded Vehicle B.S.*). However, an indoor vehicle such as a car in a garage, is also like a secret weapon, for it is an escape device hidden from common view (see *Hidden Power B.S.*). An interior vehicle is also a refuge within a refuge, and so generates a machine version of *Embedded Building B.S.* Indoor vehicles may also recall caged animals, provoking the fear of being in the lion's den.

Aircraft in hangars. Locomotives in sheds. Buses in garages. Boats in boathouses. Ships in dry dock. Transport museum exhibits. A spacecraft under wraps. Fork-lift trucks in a warehouse. A car in a living room. A buried alien craft.

Intermediate B.S.

B.S. that lies between *Primitive B.S.* and *Sophisticated B.S.*

In Transit in Parallel B.S.

B.S. generated when people or objects undertake the same journey but are separated from each other for most or all of the trip. There is a constant fear that the travellers will fail to reunite at the destination. One is tantalised by the thought of a travelling companion whom one cannot meet. This arrangement may suggest refugees fleeing in parallel but segregated by the constraints of escape. It may originate in childhood separations during journeys, but more probably reflects the archaic fear of dispersal during a panicked exodus. This could happen when members of a group flee from a predator and run off in all directions, hoping to meet up when the danger has passed. See also *Turnabout B.S.*

Airline passengers and their checked-in baggage. A ship's passenger whose furniture travels in the hold. Two friends board the same train but travel in different carriages, only meeting briefly at a station stop for coffee.

Invasion B.S.

The B.S. generated by objects arranged in patterns reminiscent of invading forces. Objects may resemble soldiers marching into battle, armoured vehicles in convoy, aircraft in formation, or a fleet of warships.

Fridges standing in rows in a shop. Free-standing paraffin heaters marching down a church aisle. Massed locomotives. Sculptures standing in a park.

Investigation B.S.

The B.S. generated when an environment is scrutinised, especially by experts. If the investigation follows an unpleasant event, *Scene of Crime B.S.* is triggered. Unexpected and B.S. relationships may be revealed through measuring devices and instruments (see *Wired-Up B.S.*). Looking beneath surfaces can generate *Dissection B.S.* and *Probe B.S.* By these processes, humdrum and quotidian things become the objects of study and are elevated to the realm of art. The everyday approximations that used to apply to the scene are replaced by an obsessive attention to detail, and things hitherto passed over become highly valued. In archaeological and forensic reconstructions, the past can be recreated, giving a frisson of *Museum B.S.*

An archaeological dig where pottery fragments (of a pot probably overlooked by its original owner) are painstakingly pieced together and displayed. A church examined for structural defects.

Laughing B.S.

This is a sad condition, despite its name, because the person in the grip of the *Laughing B.S.* loses control of many behaviours. There is unhinged laughter, an overwhelming urge to defaecate, and possibly sexual arousal as well. Each of these incontinences seems so comical and incongruous with the others that further laughter is provoked, and a vicious circle is established.

Leaving the Herd B.S.

Agitation felt when leaving the comfort of one's fellows. Leaving the herd is dangerous, since an isolated individual is more prone to attack.

Liberation B.S.

The bowel-tingling excitement at the prospect of releasing a benighted structure so that it can go off and have an adventure. It can be generated by taking a *Disappointed Structure* out of its dingy location and into the sunlight. Similarly, a *Disappointed Structure* that is a stunted version of another mechanism may be able to fulfil its potential—for example, taking an engine that has hitherto powered a factory and fitting it to a vehicle. In a sense, the object suddenly gains the prospect of a pleasant existence and escapes its prison of misery. At a more abstract level, *Liberation B.S.* is evoked by performing an important function in a venue that would normally have no hope of hosting it. Putting the spotlight on such an unlikely thing and paying it attention seems perverse but charitable and has elements of *Framing B.S.*

Taking a door from a cellar and standing it on a patio in the sunlight. Restoring an old and decrepit car that has been locked in a garage for decades and taking it for a countryside jaunt. Taking a lathe from a workshop and linking it to the drive shaft of a small trolley. Performing a play in the cellar of a terraced house. Celebrating a festival in a derelict slum.

Lightning Conductor B.S.

B.S. generated by devices that tap into elemental forces. Such devices are ambivalent, since those forces may work for or against the person harnessing them. There is a sense of wielding a fabulous weapon without having the skill or training to use it safely or effectively.

Windmills. Machines converting tidal or wave power into electricity. High-voltage generators.

Map B.S.

The B.S. generated by maps, charts, models, and other scaled representations of places or machines (see also *Model B.S.*). Maps marked with routes and safe havens echo *The Landscape of Potential Toilets*. Poring over a map is visiting a place by proxy.

A map of hostile territory. Plans of a spaceship. Architectural drawings of a large public building such as a library or hospital. A sea chart.

Minimal Camping B.S.

B.S. generated by visiting, dwelling, or working in a place while making the minimum possible impact. This involves perversely refusing to settle in or make the place feel like home. Such glancing contact also occurs in *Turnabout B.S.* Minimal camping—the refusal to put down roots—creates a feeling of being in transit, and may provoke *Travelling B.S.* or *Temporary Structure B.S.* The agitation may arise from an implied fear of predators, expressed as a reluctance to leave traces. In a sense, it avoids creating a recognisable refuge or lair that might attract unwanted attention. See also *Incognito B.S.* and *Haunter B.S.*

Buying a new house but leaving it unfurnished, sleeping in a sleeping bag and eating all meals out. Visiting a village but sleeping in a field instead of staying at the local pub.

Mobility

Defaecation reduces mobility, thereby increasing vulnerability to predation. It is striking how often mobility—and the restraint of movement—figures in *B.S. Fantasies* (see *Impeded Vehicle B.S.*). When something is both safe and mobile, it becomes especially B.S. A classic example is the flying chair, which is mobile, safe, and flies through hostile territory.

Caravans and campervans.

Model B.S.

The B.S. generated by miniature versions of objects. It may be rooted in sympathetic magic, whereby a representation and the object itself are believed to influence one another (cf. *Map B.S.*). Miniatures are easier to handle than real things, allowing danger to be toyed with safely while retaining the thrill.

Working model steam trains or beam engines. Amateur astronomical telescopes. A ship's model in the captain's quarters. Working scale models of steam engines in glass cabinets standing in the corridors of technical colleges. An architectural model of an old hospital whose roof can be removed to inspect the corridors—preferably at night, in a lit room of the real hospital (it would be too spooky to actually wander those real corridors).

Motorised B.S.

The B.S. generated by adding a motor to something that normally lacks one. The motor may suggest that the object could function as an escape vehicle (*False Vehicle B.S.*), or the incongruity may trigger a *B.S. Tension* (see *Hybrid B.S.*). Surreal combinations of normally sedentary objects with motors can be imagined, but these really belong to the realm of art.

A bookcase fitted with a petrol engine roaming a public library at night. Escalators (motorised staircases). Push-bikes with small engines. A heavy wooden desk converted into a lumbering hovercraft by strapping jet engines to its feet.

Museum B.S.

The B.S. generated by museums and museum-like exhibits, especially reconstructions of real-life situations (see *Framing B.S.*). Reconstructed rooms are particularly B.S. because they evoke *Empty Room B.S.* Museums connote dead things from the past. They may also contain impeded vehicles, especially in transport museums where old vehicles are confined indoors and may no longer function (see *Indoor Vehicle B.S.*). Museums display once-dynamic objects in stationary arrays, reminiscent of a predator's larder with carcasses.

Natural Disaster B.S.

The B.S. generated by natural disasters and, on a smaller scale, by inclement weather. There is a stark contrast between uncontrollable natural forces and the controlled and relatively weak forces of domestic life. Natural disasters such as fires, earthquakes, and floods drive animals from cover, exposing them to predators. See also *Lightning Conductor B.S.*, *Anchored B.S.* and *Gothic B.S.*

Network B.S.

The B.S. generated by communication systems linking members of a defined group (see *Telecommunications B.S.*). The response urges continued connection and inclusion, since belonging offers security. There is an implicit fear of disconnection and isolation (see *Separation from the Herd B.S.*). Networks exist at many levels: family, profession, nation, or species. Global telecommunications emphasise human unity in contrast to predators, which belong to other species.

Sending electronic mail. An obscure journal shared by those with an unusual interest.

One Way Vehicle B.S.

The B.S. generated by vehicles that are only capable of travelling in one direction. The response may warn you to be very careful about how you direct such a vehicle. The vehicle is a disposable asset: it can only be used once and offers a single opportunity for escape. It may also act as a metaphor for the progression of a person through life, since ageing is an irreversible process. *One Way Vehicle B.S.* is closely allied to *Parachute B.S.*

A rocket that jettisons stages as it climbs into space.

Out on a Limb B.S.

The B.S. generated by placing something at the far end of a structure, or by visiting the distal end of a structure (including metaphorically; see *Egregious B.S.*). At the far end, one may be conspicuous and exposed to danger. If the structure is rickety, *Unsound Structure B.S.* may also be generated. Escape usually involves retreating back along the limb, provoking *Rail B.S.* There is also the fear of being cut off at the entrance, producing the bowel-throbbing anxiety of having made a basic tactical error—like retreating into a cul-de-sac (see *Refuge-Trap B.S.*).

A restaurant at the end of a pier. Sitting or standing in a cage at the end of a mechanical arm used to service street lights or wash high windows.

Outpost B.S.

The B.S. generated by buildings or territories positioned far from the centre of an empire or its metaphorical equivalent. They are tenuously linked to the secure centre (*Umbilical Cord B.S.*) and so feel exposed to insurrection or dangerous local fauna (cf. *Distant Garden B.S.*). *Outpost B.S.* is stronger if the outpost transmits messages back to the centre, due to the addition of *Telecommunications B.S.* and *Station B.S.*

Old colonial buildings that look out of place. Forgotten backwater outposts such as small post offices or police stations. Space stations and moon bases. A radio transmitter on a distant hill.

Parachute B.S.

The B.S. generated by devices that drop you into potentially hostile territory. These one-way devices are difficult to steer. Once they have deposited their passenger, they become useless for escape. Lifts generate *Parachute B.S.* because they are capricious (and others may take control of them) and they may expose occupants to the hazards of an unknown floor. This is the final stage of *Unreliable Vehicle B.S.* and a possible consequence of *Icarian B.S.* There may be a connection with stages of our life-cycle, since we cannot backtrack (see *One Way Vehicle B.S.*). The most obvious example is being jettisoned from the cocoon of childhood. However, other organisms have more obvious parallels in their life-cycles. Trees that scatter seeds by the wind, especially sycamores, and any animal with distinct stages such as frogs that cannot revert to tadpoles, or butterflies that cannot hide again as caterpillars.

Parachutes dropped over enemy territory. Non-reusable landing vehicles used in planetary exploration.

Partition Penetrating B.S.

Partitions have strong *B.S. Gradients*, so structures that penetrate them—and link disparate spaces—are very B.S. They are like wires that connect zones of different voltage.

Windows, portals, spyholes, laundry chutes, chimneys, lift shafts, dumbwaiters, paternoster lifts, and periscopes.

Pioneering B.S.

B.S. generated by activities that open up new territory—physical, artistic, or intellectual. A feeling of being out on the rim. See *Egregious B.S., Edge of the Herd B.S.* and *Out on a Limb B.S.*

Building a house in virgin territory. Creating an artwork that fits no existing classification. Working on a new theory.

Pole B.S.

Poles and stilts are B.S. because they lift people or objects clear of the ground, reducing the threat of attack while increasing visibility—you can see and be seen more easily from the top of a pole (*Refuge-Trap B.S.*), a classic *B.S. Paradox*. Displaying an object on a pole generates *Framing B.S.* Poles amplify the B.S. of other objects and are useful in *B.S. Fantasies*. They may recall ancestral tree refuges, although trees now carry too many associations to remain purely B.S. Poles often look fragile and provoke *Unreliable Machine B.S.*

Tree houses. Piers. A car on a pole. A telephone on a pole in the middle of a park lake. Buildings on stilts. Walking across a mill pond at night on stilts. Marching across a planet on robotic stilts.

Portal B.S.

The discomfiture generated by lingering in entranceways. Hovering in doorways, porches, hatches, man-
holes, portholes, and the like is B.S., because one is exposed to exterior threats from one side but protected on
the other. Portals allow the ingress of predators and enemies, but at the same time offer an escape hatch—an
example of a *B.S. Paradox*. Objects that straddle doorways—connecting the interior of a building with the outside, and preventing the door from closing—are excruciatingly B.S., since a huge *B.S. Gradient* runs through
them. See *Partition Penetrating B.S.*

*Sitting in a wooden chair in a doorway with your back to
the outside world. Sitting on a spindly metal chair that
projects halfway above a manhole cover in the middle of
the road on a damp Tuesday night.*

Post-Holocaust B.S.

The B.S. generated in the aftermath of a disaster. There
may be a fear that something horrendous is still lurking
about, or that some invader will move in to fill the power
vacuum created by the absence of people (see *Empty City
B.S.*). There is a powerful sense of transformation, which
is always unsettling, and a disturbing feeling that something irrevocable has happened.

Wandering around a city after the bomb has gone off.

Primitive B.S.

The most basic kind of B.S., generated by fear of enemies or predators. It produces a simple urge to defaecate.

Primitive Machine B.S.

B.S. generated by machines with primitive or unstreamlined designs. *Primitive Machine B.S.* is partly due to the large number of details (see *Detail B.S.*) and the obvious working parts (see *External Mechanism B.S.*). Primitive machines may resemble experimental prototypes that have not been proven to work, and fear of them failing might provoke *Unreliable Machine B.S.* or *Icarian B.S.* They might also look weak and so generate *Inadequate Machine B.S.* Strange appendages and decorations could make a machine look insectile, and so provoke a fear of other creatures. *Primitive Machine B.S.* may be a protective response to key characteristics of ancient predators. In other words, when we see a machine with fins, plates, jointed appendages and bulbous outgrowths, and decorated with bumps, ridges and spikes, it churns our bowels because we are responding to cues that were present in predators that lived millions of years ago.

Vintage motorbikes. Cars with fins and running boards. Valve amplifiers with cooling fins.

Probe B.S.

The B.S. generated by investigative devices that inspect distant, dangerous, or inaccessible places where enemies or predators may lurk. All probes remain connected in some way to their operator. Some probes have a physical connection such as a wire or tube, whereas others use a radio signal or laser beam. Consequently, enemies or predators may notice the probe and follow it back to you. The fear of enemies tracking along a mechanism to reach you occurs in *External Mechanism B.S. Probe B.S.* may therefore be a warning against advertising your presence to potentially hostile life-forms (see also *Remote Control B.S.*). Probes also allow you to visit dangerous places by proxy, whilst you are safe in a refuge.

Periscopes that scan the surface waters from a submarine. Space probes that return pictures from distant and inhospitable planets. Robots that go to the bottom of the sea or into volcanoes. Interplanetary probes that return soil samples from cold moons.

Proximity to Traffic B.S.

B.S. generated by nearby vehicles and roads. It may work by eliciting the *Travelling B.S.* by proxy. However, traffic may carry enemies or offer a means of escape (see *Station B.S.*). Public footpaths next to houses create this effect.

Coffee shops at bus interchanges. Restaurants in motorway flyovers. A lounge room adjacent to a thoroughfare.

Proximity to Water B.S.

B.S. generated by nearby bodies of water that might contain submerged predators. It may hark back to an ancient aquatic existence, when our marine forebears had to evade underwater predators. Even when our ancestors conquered the land, the association between water and attack remained because watering holes provide rich pickings for predators. The drinker is still vulnerable to attack from the water (e.g. from crocodilians) and to attack from behind, from the land (e.g. from big cats). As if the mix of aquatic, amphibious, and terrestrial predators is not enough, the watering hole usually lacks cover. Still waters, such as moats and millponds, seem particularly bowel stirring. See also *Diluvian B.S.* and *Feeding B.S.*

Canals near a house. The ocean viewed through a glass-bottomed boat. Loch Ness. Wells, especially dilapidated ones.

Rail B.S.

B.S. generated by restrictive vehicular guides, such as railways, tramways, the cables that support cable cars, and chutes. Like roads you cannot leave, rails highlight an avenue of escape but do not allow you to deviate from it. The escape route is easy to see but difficult to leave. They are also visible to the enemy or predator, making them a trap as well as an escape route (see *Refuge-Trap B.S.*). On a railway, there is an underlying fear of ambush. *Rail B.S.* might also work because they make routes explicit, which is one mechanism in the B.S. assessment of terrain; see *The Landscape of Potential Toilets*.

Re-Cycling B.S.

B.S. generated by contemplating the original incarnation of the materials that make up an object. This creates a link with a different object or period (see *Temporal B.S.*). There may also be a tension between the original material and the use to which it is now put. Certain forms of *B.S. Art* may work in this way. Re-cycling may also have biological connotations, such as the conversion of foodstuffs to body structures. Dead bodies may rot in the soil and so re-cycle into vegetation.

Refuge-Trap B.S.

B.S. generated by the fear that a refuge might turn into a trap, or even be a disguised trap. This may be a central mechanism of the B.S., since recognising hidden traps or dead ends helps us to survive.

Remote Control B.S.

B.S. generated by machines (in the broadest sense) that can be remotely controlled. Such devices can be used in hostile or inaccessible places, without risking the safety of the human operator. The B.S. arises because the controller ventures into hostile territory by proxy (see *Probe B.S.*).

Rotating Building B.S.

B.S. generated when part of a building rotates. Related to *Motorised B.S.*, since buildings are normally immobile.

Observatories in which the dome and telescope rotate to scan the heavens. A revolving restaurant at the top of a tower. A windmill.

Scene of Crime B.S.

The B.S. triggered by contemplating the scene of a crime. More generally, the discomfiture generated by contemplating the scene of an outbreak, be it of violence, pollution, or infection. There is the fear that the criminal may return to the scene, or that some toxic residue remains, or that an infection still poses a threat. The cordoning off of the scene and the careful search for clues generate *Investigation B.S.* Because the scene was transfigured and rendered extraordinary, it generates *Framing B.S.*

A murder scene. An environmental disaster. A house contaminated and unfit for habitation. A hospital suffering an outbreak of a lethal infection.

Secret Passage B.S.

Secret passages and rooms offer concealment and physical protection, and a delicious sense of hiding from the world. This thrill is akin to the childhood delight of playing hide-and-seek, and strongly suggests a childhood origin for this type of B.S. Secret passages make good escape routes, although invaders can also use them. This double-edged quality is a common theme in the B.S. See *B.S. Paradox, Refuge-Trap B.S.* and *External Mechanism B.S.*

Separate Structure B.S.

B.S. generated by small refuges near larger ones. In the lesser refuge, one may feel a bowel-throbbing urge to dash for the larger and (presumably) more secure refuge. At the same time, one might be reluctant to quit the smaller refuge since it is known to be safe, whereas the larger one might harbour hostile things (see *Embedded Building B.S.*). This is another example of a *B.S. Paradox.*

A sentry box beyond the railings of a large house or palace. A potting shed in a garden. A small boat bobbing around near a large ship.

Separation from the Herd B.S.

B.S. generated by the anxiety of being separated from one's fellows. This is a very dangerous situation, since predators often seek to isolate an animal from the rest of the herd.

Sitting B.S.

B.S. generated by sitting. Sitting reduces mobility, making escape more difficult. It is also harder to keep a lookout in all directions (for this reason, *Sitting B.S.* can be intensified by facing a wall). There is a bowel agitation in knowing that you are a sitting target. Sitting or squatting also suggests defaecation, and this immobility is one of the roots of the B.S. *Sitting B.S.* can be elicited by a chair in an exposed or unexpected place. A swing offers an interesting form of *Sitting B.S.*, since its movements might suggest it is a vehicle (see *Impeded Vehicle B.S.*). Rocking chairs, too, have a hint of the vehicular, and this might explain why they feature in films to create tension. Swinging and rocking back and forth in the chair suggest not only impediment, but an attempt to break free. Unoccupied rocking chairs that rock hint at an invisible occupant—or even a swaying, mantis-like predator.

Sitting in a corridor. A chair in the street or on a railway platform. A swing hung in a doorway. A rocking chair in an attic.

Skeletal B.S.

B.S. generated by an open-work structure. There is a heightened sense of exposure in a framework (one is literally framed and presented, inviting inspection). This creates the bowel-tingling sense of being in a cage or trap, awaiting the predator. Skeletal structures also suggest the remains of a dead animal, implying a nearby predator.

Standing in the wooden framework of a house under construction. Looking down at the sea through the slats of a pier. Swimming around the skeleton-like remains of a shipwreck. Viewing the world from a playpen.

Specialised Mechanism B.S.

B.S. generated by devices designed for a specialised job. They are uncompromisingly utilitarian (see *Task B.S.*) and may have strange arms, dials, and other appendages that trigger *Primitive Machine B.S.* and *External Mechanism B.S.* They seem at ease in their natural environments, but outside they look orphaned and vulnerable. Being so specialised, they cannot cope in a hostile setting, like an exotic specimen escaped from a menagerie, and so might perish. The sense of them being restricted by their specialism may also trigger *Disappointed Structure B.S.* Specialised devices are rarer than general-purpose ones, and may therefore seem predatory (predators are rarer than prey). Their predatory mien is amplified by all the levers and controls.

Mechanical diggers parked beside a road. Printing presses standing in a field. Tractors in transit. Rickety production lines in old factories. Bizarre and archaic scientific instruments.

Staircase B.S.

B.S. associated with stairs. Stairs are for purposeful climbing, so lingering on them generates the B.S. Dawdling in places that are intended for determined travellers is always B.S., like sitting in the middle of a racetrack or a hospital corridor. Stairs are literal *B.S. Gradients* because they join floors that have different comfort levels. Sometimes higher storeys seem more secure (our forebears were safer in a tree); at other times, less (it is harder to escape from an upper storey)—a *B.S. Paradox*. Children are fascinated by stairs, and adults may find them B.S. because of childhood recollections. Being narrow guides, stairs may also elicit *Rail B.S.*

Sitting halfway up the stairs in a deserted technical college.

Station B.S.

B.S. generated by stations of any kind. In this book, stations are seen as reliable and predictable structures through which traffic flows. They are still—literally stationary—compared with their associated traffic, which sets up a huge *B.S. Tension*. The traffic can be anything: water (as in a pump station), information (as in a relay station), trains (as in a railway station), or mail (as in a post office). *Station B.S.* combines a sense of security (stations are relatively secure, permanent and still) with a fear of being left behind (the traffic that leaves them) and in some cases a fear of what might arrive at them—a dangerous passenger on the next train, or an assassin on the next plane. The fear of arrivals is strong because stations are destinations for passengers and are therefore obvious targets for things that prey on travellers. Stations are also reminiscent of the refuges that appear on escape routes (see *The Landscape of Potential Toilets*). Being stationary, they trigger *Sitting B.S.*

Sitting on a small collapsible stool in a bus terminal at midnight. Waiting on a deserted railway platform in the middle of nowhere. Standing in the sorting room of a post office watching letters and parcels flow through. Airports.

Supernatural B.S.

B.S. generated by supernatural beings, events, or forces. Such things are like super-predators which, apart from being powerful, might not respond to conventional weapons or rational entreaties.

Supervention by Machine B.S.

B.S. generated by a fear of being replaced by robots—a fear of having entered a machine realm in which we no longer belong.

Traffic lights changing on a deserted road late at night, especially in the wet. Automatic production lines.

Task B.S.

B.S. generated by having to perform a task. Doing a job usually means keeping still and concentrating—the consequent reduction in mobility and lowering one's guard increase the risk of attack. Many *B.S. Fantasies* are enhanced by introducing a task. Workplaces are symbols of tasks (in the same way that chairs are symbols of sitting) and so tend to be bowel stirring.

Writing letters in the back bedroom of a deserted house. Mending a clock in a cellar. Doing homework in a deserted school. A factory at night.

Telecommunications B.S.

B.S. generated by equipment used in telecommunications (including broadcasting), its associated buildings, and other paraphernalia. Telecommunication equipment connects distant points, creating a *B.S. Gradient*, like a wire connecting two regions of different voltage. Telecommunication devices can summon help (a cry to others in the herd), transmit warnings (of dangers threatening the herd), enable conversation (kinship), and rally the herd (cohesion). Telecommunicating may, paradoxically, remind us of our isolation (see *Egregious B.S.* and *Outpost B.S.*).

Making a telephone call from a box on a windy street corner. Standing near a radio mast on top of a mountain at night. Tuning an old radio to a distant station. Watching television in a classroom in a deserted technical college. Communicating with Earth from a distant planet.

Temporal B.S.

B.S. associated with time—especially the past—or with time travel. Generated by the contrast between the present and some other period. Sometimes, the present seems less secure because it is unpredictable, whereas the past is immutable. In other instances, the present seems relatively safer than an unknown period (time travel exploits this fear of other times). *Temporal B.S.* is closely related to the pangs of nostalgia and an urge to return to the security of childhood.

Browsing through an attic full of old things. Imagining wandering the streets of your childhood. Time machines. Clocks. Museums.

Temporary Structure B.S.

B.S. generated by temporary buildings or other short-lived structures. The knowledge that such structures—especially if they are refuges—will be dismantled is very unsettling because the B.S. warns us to make other arrangements for our future. Temporary structures tend to be weaker than permanent ones and so generate a version of *Inadequate Machine B.S.* akin to *Unsound Structure B.S.* This B.S. may have originated in our nomadic ancestors who regularly set up and dismantled their camps.

Temporary offices. Tents. Amplification equipment set up for a rock concert. Lights, cameras and dressing rooms set up for location filming. Investigation equipment set up around a crime scene or an archaeological site.

Tower B.S.

B.S. generated by towers, especially derelict ones. Towers usually imply some degree of fortification (refuge) and offer a commanding view. Towers that have fallen into disrepair therefore generate a potent *False Refuge B.S.* Like poles (see *Pole B.S.*), towers are ambivalent structures: they offer security but may display their occupant for all to see, creating a *B.S. Paradox.*

Travelling B.S.

Intense urge to defaecate before a journey. The longer the trip, or the more hostile the route or destination, the more intense the feeling. It originates in the urge to pre-emptively void the bowels before venturing into hazardous terrain. This B.S. may be combined with constipation when away. Some people experience both effects and can therefore timetable their motions to occur at home.

Trespass B.S.

B.S. generated by illicitly entering territory that belongs to another. There may be real physical danger from an enemy or predator, or a lesser danger from a higher-ranking member of the same tribe (rifling through the boss's office). In *B.S. Fantasies, Trespass B.S.* can be combined with invisibility to great effect (see *Incognito B.S.* and *Haunter B.S.*).

Turnabout B.S.

B.S. generated by intentionally ignoring the obvious reason for a visit. The discomfiture arises because a refuge is perversely bypassed during a long trip. Far from the comfort of home, the B.S. urges you to enter the obvious refuge. In *Turnabout B.S.*, one may feel like a poorly directed probe or remotely controlled machine. It may also have its roots in truancy, when one might take the day off school but instead of going to play, one sits outside the school gate or hides in a deserted classroom. *Turnabout B.S.* can be enjoyed by a group of people who arrange to be in the same place at the same time but avoid all contact with each other. The more distant the meeting place, the better. They may or may not remain hidden from each other. Such perverse non-meetings are exceedingly pure B.S. exercises. See also *In Transit in Parallel B.S.*

Travelling back in time to your childhood but only walking down neighbouring streets (avoiding your old home). Trav-

elling back in time to your junior school but avoiding your own class. Landing on the moon and going to sleep, rather than getting out and having a look round. Travelling half-way around the world and then staying in a house one block away from your family and returning without visiting them. Arranging a non-convention in a foreign hotel, in which all the delegates avoid each other completely.

Umbilical B.S.

Tenuous connections to a refuge generate this type of B.S. (see *Anchored B.S.*). The bowel stirring response warns us to be vigilant, lest the metaphorical or mechanical umbilical cord be cut. The cord can take many forms and may echo our natal expulsion into the hostile unknown. External umbilical devices—for example, the line tethering a spacewalker to the spacecraft—also generate *External Mechanism B.S.*

A telephone line. A crane that suspends you over dangerous territory. A corridor connecting a safe room to the exterior. The lifeline from a boat to a diver.

Unreliable Machine B.S.

Unreliable machines can leave you exposed if you rely on them for protection or escape. They can break down just when you need them. However, they titillate with the promise of protection. A very similar gut warning occurs in *Inadequate Machine B.S., False Refuge B.S., False Vehicle*

B.S., Impeded Vehicle B.S., Unreliable Vehicle B.S., and *Refuge-Trap B.S.* Machines that fail like this sometimes figure in ghost stories. They belong to the everyday world and signal an entry into another realm when they fail. Under the right circumstances, any machine can evoke *Unreliable Machine B.S.* (for example, even the most robust or high-tech equipment can fail against supernatural forces).

Torches that fail. Weapons that run out of ammunition. Weapons whose power supply fails.

Unreliable Refuge B.S.

Refuges that might fail to protect are disturbing. The B.S. acts as a warning not to rely on such places for security.

A telephone box with a broken door.

Unreliable Vehicle B.S.

Unreliable vehicles are an important category of *Unreliable Machines*. They are B.S. because they suggest the possibility of escape but cannot deliver.

A flying machine that can only hover when you need it to soar. A crippled spacecraft trying to leave a hostile planet. An open-top car that can only limp away from a crowd of zombies.

Unsound Structure B.S.

B.S. generated by a fear that a building or other structure will collapse. The B.S. acts as a warning to quit the structure. It may have originated to protect us from venturing onto parts of a tree that could not support us, or onto ground that could give way.

A tumble-down house or factory.

Wired-Up B.S.

B.S. generated by exposed or untidily placed wires, cables, and instruments. It is especially strong when equipment is being fitted or set up temporarily. Equipment installed for a particular job generates a visible form of *Task B.S.* Wires strewn about change our reaction to a place, since they highlight various features and reveal unexpected relationships. The location may seem prepped for a detailed inspection, triggering *Investigation B.S.* A wired-up place can feel intimidating; it might evoke a decorated lair (see *Trespass B.S.*) or a wiry trap, like a spider's web. Wires and other components can look vaguely anatomical and suggest a partly dissected body (see *Dissection B.S.*).

Re-wiring a house. Fitting a telephone network in an office. Installing a television studio. Filming in a public place.

Wolf in Sheep's Clothing B.S.

The B.S. arising from something dangerous masquerading as something friendly and safe.

A warship disguised as a merchant ship.

Afterword

THAT WAS THE BOOK as finished in 1996, with some light editing for flow, formatting, spelling, and grammar. Think of it as a classic car abandoned in a garage for thirty years—now cleaned, polished, and serviced. With a new carburettor. And fresh wiper blades. Restored in this way, the 1996 manuscript becomes a B.S. artefact in its own right. Bracketing the exhumed work with an introduction and this afterword creates temporal tension and a textbook case of *Framing B.S.*

Examining *Bowel Stirring Things* as an unearthed time capsule produces a species of forensic B.S. with a faint hint of archaeology. Lost. Liminal. Nostalgic.

Remember: B.S. is trepidation in the face of a suspected trap—an ancient predator-detection heuristic. Walk its alleyways, if you dare.

Good luck.